L.M. BASSETT

MARCH 1978

Rags
to
Righteousness

Rags to Righteousness

by Gordon M. Hyde

Pacific Press Publishing Association
Mountain View, California
Omaha, Nebraska
Oshawa, Ontario

Copyright © 1978 by
Pacific Press Publishing Association
Litho in United States of America
All Rights Reserved
Library of Congress Card No. 77-80684

Contents

1.Prolgue

In a stately old English mansion I served at tables, but I was not the butler, not even the liveried footman. As I stood tray in hand at my post by the hatchway to the enormous kitchen, I kept rolling off my tongue an idea that had the taste of a choice morsel. To me it was new and almost unbelievable. Over and over it came like the incessant waves on the beaches of England: "Now look, Christ is my righteousness." "His righteousness is mine." "I am righteous by faith in Him."

My monologue went on like that for days. Whether in the morning and evening worships, in chapel, during the weekend services, in classes, or on the job—waiting at tables there in the student dining room that had once been the Palm House—it was everywhere the same, the constantly repeated theme of my mind. My faith wanted so desperately to dare to reach out and take hold of God's promises, wanted to claim as mine His "precious and very great promises" (2 Peter 1:4, R.S.V.), wanted to feel the lightening of the load of guilt and despair that came with my often-repeated promises and resolutions that always led equally to often-repeated failures. And every time my heart, my mind, dared to reach out to claim these promises as mine, it was as though the sun had struggled through the mist and gloom of a bleak, foggy, midwinter day in the midst of old England.

I hardly sensed it then, but I was on the very edge of my own personal discovery of what millions of followers of the Lord Jesus had learned before me: "Since we are justified by faith, we have peace with God through our Lord Jesus Christ." Romans 5:1, R.S.V. And such peace! Deep, quiet, personal, sometimes singing, vibrating peace—under the smile of God. Relief, release, deliverance, joy, real joy, wonderful joy!

It is for you.

It had been struggle enough to be up, showered, shaved, and shirted before the 6:45 a.m. worship bell when we first enrolled for the autumn term at Newbold College, an estate with its rolling acres in the heart of the leafy county of Warwickshire in the English Midlands. The three of us friends had the urge to do something special. We wanted to do better, go an extra mile—or two if need be. We had to get right with God, had to have the assurance of being righteous, of doing right. Even dared to hope we could get to where we wouldn't be sinning anymore. But how could we do that without prayer? We must pray more, must read the Bible more. We just had to try harder to please the Lord, to measure up to all His requirements. So push the alarm clock half an hour earlier. Dress before the lights come on, before the heat, clanging and chattering in the old steam pipes, had taken the raw edge off the damp cold of the night.

Out the back door of the men's dorm, across sweeping beech-shaded lawns, past the old boathouse, and into the long, wooded "spinney" (thicket) to a rustic shelter with its creaky door. There, by the light of a "torch" (flashlight) we would read and we would pray.

Then back to the routine of a school day, trying harder, sometimes remembering the prayer of the morning, perhaps recalling a fragment of a promise read. Coming swiftly to the end of a short winter day. Looking back. Checking, wondering. Then deciding, with a deepening glow of self-satisfaction: "I don't think I have sinned today. Can't think of anything I have said or done wrong today. Must be making progress. Maybe I'll make it yet. Soon I'll get to where I don't sin anymore. I'll get to be righteous."

It began to occur to me sometimes that the apostle Paul had not very much up on me. I remembered how he said, "I myself have reason for confidence in the flesh also. If any other man thinks he has reason for confidence in the flesh, I have more: circumcised on the eighth day, of the people of Israel, of the tribe of Benjamin, a Hebrew born of Hebrews; as to the law a Pharisee, as to zeal a persecutor of the church, as to righteousness under the law blameless." Philippians 3:4-6, R.S.V.

I could write something like that. Son of pioneer believers in the Advent message in the British Isles. Father a cornet player and Mother a singer and tambourinist in the Salvation Army. Both of them witnessing on the street corners of old London. Brought into "the message" by a crippled layman who rode a donkey cart as he sold the English *Present Truth* from door to door. Father losing his bakery business on his decision to close his shop on the Saturday Sabbath—busiest baker's day of all the week. Youngest son of a large family of Seventh-day Adventist workers, I had six brothers and six sisters. Five of the sons ordained ministers. Three sisters married to ministers. All of the girls somewhere sometime engaged in "the Lord's work." Three brothers had given

themselves to the service of Africa—pioneering service.
(One of them resting early in a missionary's grave in the
heart of old Solusi Mission.) Baptized by the world-
renowned author and editor Uncle Arthur Maxwell.
And now, here I was in training for the ministry. And
getting a little better every day. Quite a little better, in
fact!

And we had some other claims to righteousness. In
the interest of the body temple, in our home we were all
vegetarians. (Not all Christians could claim that.) In our
home we were accustomed to family worship. (Not
every Christian family could claim that.) Our parents
were meticulously faithful in their payment of tithe on
their rather limited income, and Dad was so generous
with offerings that Mother sometimes questioned his
liberality with "the cause" when the needs of his own
large family were so great and so many. (It wasn't every
Christian family that could boast of that.) And oh, yes, to
come to think of it, my Father had been a worker for a
short time at the denominational "Jerusalem" in Battle
Creek, Michigan, where with a baker's training he had
studied the health food business in the days of Dr. J. H.
Kellogg. So he had met or had heard many of the
pioneers of the Seventh-day Adventist Church. Yes, I
could write quite a religious pedigree somewhat com-
parable to that of the apostle Paul.

So there was a strong basis for the temptation to religious smugness and self-assurance. In fact there may
not have been a lot of difference between some of my
prayers and those of the Pharisee in Christ's parable who
thanked God that he was not as other men and who
proceeded to provide the Lord with a catalog of his
personal virtues and his religious practices which he
thought should entitle him to acceptance with God.

Oh, yes, and I could point with some degree of pride to the virtue of a decision that I had recently made when I had the choice of going to teacher training at an English State College or of attending Newbold and preparing for the ministry. Needless to say I had made the "right decision" in choosing God's school at Newbold over a "worldly" school of teacher training. Really my halo was not only beautifully adjusted but it was brilliant, brilliant with self-righteousness.

You wouldn't need prophetic insight to know that this "sainty" young man in training at Newbold College was building up for one enormous letdown. And it came so easily, so softly, so painfully easily. One evening after worship, my girl friend, troubled by my growing "Christian" self-confidence, and protesting by contrast her own spiritual inadequacy, broke down in an outburst of tears declaring her hopeless condition. Whereupon she fled up the staircase to the girl's section of the dormitory; and I, normally knowing better, tried to follow her to protest her protestations and to bring her back. There was a sharp voice of remonstrance and a restraining hand from the dean of men who just had to happen by, and I turned on him in anger, pouring out a torrent of words over the gross injustice and lack of sympathy and understanding that he was manifesting. And suddenly I knew that my beautiful rainbow-hued bubble of self-righteousness had simply popped in my face. And that a simple little trip-up to my stately religious steppings had been quite enough to send me down to levels of despair and self-condemnation only matched by my earlier smug sense of spiritual adequacy.

The first reasoned reaction was to ask: What's the use? The higher you climb, the farther you fall. So why not forget it all and be content to muddle along as an "average good Christian" and hope to muddle through with the rest of them to the kingdom?

It was just about then and there that a particular man in the dorm all unknowingly had begun to gain my attention and arouse my curiosity. I had always had a special liking for Europeans ("Continentals" as we called them in England), perhaps because my own Father had been born in Germany and had come as an immigrant to England as a boy of fourteen to be apprenticed to his German-baker uncle in the great city of London. And often during my growing-up years our home had echoed to the intriguing accents and persistent efforts of visiting European students to speak English. But there was more than my regular interest in this particular European student. He was older than most of us in the first place, and he spoke even less English than the average "Continental" coming to Newbold. His accent was heavier if anything, and his speech more halting. But it was what he was doing that intrigued me. Since I had already had a summer or two selling religious books, plus weekends during school term, I couldn't believe that here was a man who could scarcely talk one straight sentence of English (and who was taking part-time schoolwork in order to learn English); yet, when not in classes, he was out *selling* religious books in the villages surrounding Newbold— villages in which we had sold books when the college first moved there but which had become weary of our calling and resistant to our selling. And he was selling bigger and more expensive books than most of us ever handled. I was fascinated to know how this man could sell anything with his halting language.

For another thing, I noticed how thoroughly he prepared for the coming of the Sabbath day. He would not go out selling on Friday afternoon; but after lunch he would put on old togs, thoroughly clean his room, shine his shoes, get his laundry, and press his suit. By the setting of the sun he would be sitting in his room, his face spread with a beatific smile, awaiting the coming of the Sabbath day of rest. I was impressed.

Then one Sabbath afternoon I happened across him in the commons room. He was reading—some books in English, some in German—for he had come from Schleswig-Holstein and German was his main language. I broke in to ask what he was reading. He passed the book over to me as he said, "Luther's *Commentary on Galatians.* Vonderful book. Same spirit here as in best Adventist books," he assured me. In my ignorance and prejudice I could not conceive such a thing, and I drifted off.

But the man with the easy smile and the calm confidence of one who walks with God kept breaking in on my attention without his saying a word to me. And it was ultimately from him that I learned a truth which had never registered with me in my nineteen years of living in a godly home and attending the headquarters church. It was the fact that Christ is *my* righteousness. I learned that this was the basis of this man's calm assurance, of his joyous and victorious outlook on life with its vicissitudes. I began to see why he might sell books where we couldn't. I was tremendously impressed. Here he seemed to be living the way I wanted so much to live. Yet he seemed to be doing it with quiet joy, almost effortlessly and certainly without one trace of the smug Pharisaism that said to others, "I am better than you." Thus this humble man with little formal education, a

14

blacksmith by trade, who manifested a depth of wisdom and understanding beyond anything that I could remember having met before, led me as by the hand into the pathway of the righteousness of Jesus Christ.

My soul found peace and rest. It also found great significance in what Luther once said—that a man seldom finds righteousness by faith who has not had a persistent and arduous struggle to obtain righteousness by works. And as I looked back, I could sense my struggle to be righteous by my own works from the days that I first learned to distinguish between right and wrong.

It began to occur to me as something strange and hard to explain that none of my Bible teachers at college, or my Sabbath School teachers back through the years, or any of the pastors of the home church, or visiting speakers, or my own beloved and devout parents had managed to convey to me (although they may actually have known and understood the matter for themselves) that the righteousness, the obedience, the perfection which Jesus Christ practiced in His life here on this earth could be counted to me as though I had lived that way. When I was ready to forsake all confidence in myself and my own record of attempted righteousness and place my full weight of trust and confidence in His righteousness, then it was counted to me for righteousness.

I found myself wondering what position my church really took on this matter of justification by faith. Why had I not picked it up early in my childhood and boyhood connection with the church and my own family? Why had I not discerned it in the preaching of my pastors at the denominational headquarters church for the British Isles? We listened to some outstanding preachers, consecrated men. I loved them dearly and respected them thoroughly, and it was they who led me on to my own baptism into Christ and into the church—His body. (Maybe it was I who could not hear what they were trying to tell.)

Here again, it was my newfound Continental friend who was able to call my attention to a book written in the twenties by a man who for many years served as one of the most outstanding presidents of the General Conference of Seventh-day Adventists, Arthur G. Daniells. And the little book was entitled *Christ Our Righteousness*. I was so excited by some of the things which I read in a borrowed copy that I hastily ordered one and duly underlined almost every line in red ink! I wondered where this book had been since its publication and why I had never heard of it before.

In this small volume I not only gained confirmation of my new personal experience in claiming Christ as my righteousness but learned that this emphasis had been a matter of issue if not of crisis in the history of my church around the year 1888—the year especially remembered for the General Conference session that was held in Minneapolis, Minnesota, in the autumn of that year.

Amid the ninety or so delegates there were strong and almost bitter cleavages, with some accepting the message of justification by faith with real joy, and some opposing it as the undermining of the mission and message of Seventh-day Adventists, and others holding a mutual ground and awaiting further developments.

But the excitement of my personal discovery was only slightly tempered by my reading of the controversy and conflict that had been created in the past by the same message of truth that was beginning to absorb my thought and attention.

So what do you do when you have made the greatest discovery of your young life? Do you show the discretion, discernment, and tact of the experienced? Not a chance. You want to show it to everybody you meet —anybody you think might be remotely interested. You write home about it, you talk to your closest friends about it, you talk to your teachers about it. Some are delighted and accepting. Some are troubled. And some are definitely opposed.

It struck me first as something strange that the new sense of release from the burden of striving to make myself righteous (and to measure up to all the requirements and involvements of God's holy, moral, Ten Commandment law) gave me also the greatest desire and motivation for doing God's will that I had ever experienced. I found myself, for example, writing letters of apology for past offenses, letters of restitution over things which had slipped back in my memory but which now came clearly forward demanding attention. It was not a burden to face these new obligations but a joy. It was not long either before many new lessons of life and of Christian faith thrust themselves upon me. It soon became evident that observers may take exception to new theological positions or understandings of the Scriptures advocated by some. However, the opposition to such is as nothing compared with the reaction that comes when an individual not only *believes* a little differently but begins to *act* and *behave* differently. This reaction was conspicuous when other students came in contact with and learned from my new Continental friend (and who even condescended to listen to my own feeble witness to the message of righteousness by faith) and very quickly began to change their habits and some aspects of their life-styles. Some who had been ram-

bunctious and extremely extrovert in dress and man-
nerisms became much more quiet and temperate. Facts
which they had long known about better ways of main-
taining the health and strength of the body temple began
to be practiced rather than to be held merely as interesting theories.

In a school that about lived on bread and jam and hot
drink (duly sweetened) it just could not be inconspicu-
ous that a dozen or more students had begun to abandon
the sugary hot drinks and the sugar-ladened jams and
jellies of a typical English table. When students begin to
turn down biscuits and cakes along with puddings and
the ever-present Bird's custard, then conspicuousness is
absolutely inevitable. In this case the reaction was often
not pleasant or happy. A lot of razzing developed, and
taunts of being "sainty" or "holy" began to fly around.
How desperately those involved needed the encouragement and yet moderating counsel of those of maturer
years of experience that they might know when to speak
and when to be silent and how to move graciously, yet
cautiously, in order to minimize resistance and criti-
cism.

In spite of all, in proportion to the size of the student
body, a conspicuous number of young people caught
the flame of justification by faith from one another, and
among these were some of the most capable students in
the school.

This brief account of a real-life experience has been
assembled under the caption "Prologue," and really
that is exactly what it is intended to be—a prologue to
the study of the Bible in the following chapters. There
the Word will shed the light of revelation and inspira-
tion upon the issues illustrated in this chapter. It

seemed to me that the presentation of the truths of salvation in a true-to-life setting might assure the reader that
the subject of this book is not mere theory. And it is not
theology alone, though it is that. But it is the key to a
vital and real experience *with* Christ and *in* Christ, and it
touches deeply upon the simplest and commonest aspects of real everyday living. From here we will move on
to a consideration of the steps people usually take who
have had the joy of coming to Jesus Christ for the salvation which He so abundantly offers.

2.What Must I Do?

With respect to salvation, the most persistent issue that has faced the Seventh-day Adventist Church in its comparatively short history is wrapped up in the simple question, What must I do to be saved?

The answers given over the years of Seventh-day Adventist history to this basic and biblical question, if analyzed and reduced to their simplest possible terms, would include three factors:

1. Man cannot save himself from the pit of sin in which he finds himself (by factors of both inheritance and his own willful ways). Therefore, his only and all-sufficient hope of salvation is found in responding to the love of God in Christ Jesus, whose righteousness is offered to the individual believer as the sole and all-sufficient basis for his being, and continuing to be, acceptable to God as a candidate for the kingdom in which will dwell only righteousness.

2. Since man cannot save himself, his only hope of salvation at the outset is in responding to the love of God in Christ Jesus. This he does by accepting the righteousness of Christ as the sole basis of his salvation. Then having accepted this saving act of God in Christ Jesus, he must go on in the way of salvation and particularly in

the way of sanctification to become more and more completely and perfectly obedient to the will of God (as outlined in the Ten Commandments and lived by Jesus Christ when here on earth). If he lives to see Christ's second coming, he must have reached by or before then a state or condition in which he no longer disobeys in any respect the will of God. If he fails to measure up over this long-term pull toward what many would rather generally call "perfection" (moral perfection, sinless perfection and any other variables on that concept), then—in spite of the faith that he has had the righteousness of Christ counted to him for righteousness and even in spite of the fact that he has recognized that he cannot achieve perfection by his own strength alone (but must be open to and cooperative with the indwelling Holy Spirit bringing the presence of the Father and of the Son into the life)—all this will avail him nothing and he will ultimately be lost. (An unspoken logical corollary to this would seem to be that one would be fortunate if he should die before the general close of human probation and the pronouncement of the decree which finalizes the life record of every human being who has ever lived on the face of the earth. In such a case he could be saved by his faith in the righteousness of Christ counted to him for righteousness, even though he was in some respects falling short of God's perfect ideal for His children at the time of death.)

3. There may be another variable on the second alternative which has just been presented, in that some might wish to say that God's overruling providence and the work of the Holy Spirit will see to it that those who wholeheartedly desire perfection will be preserved and brought to that blessed state by the time human probation closes.

Each of these three alternatives undoubtedly has variables and possibly distortions. But, taken together, these variables represent a major theological, doctrinal, and experiential issue within the ranks of Adventism. This can be readily documented both currently and in the history of the church, whether one wishes to think of the Palmdale "righteousness by faith statement" appearing in the *Review and Herald* (with the authority of the church paper) in its issue of May 27, 1976; or of the appeals for revival and reformation from the world session of the church at Vienna in the summer of 1975 and the preceding Annual Councils of the General Conference Committee in 1973 and 1974; or of going back to such publications as A. G. Daniells's book, *Christ Our Righteousness*, first issued in 1926. Other denominational publications have also dealt with the subject: A. W. Spalding's two-volume history of the denomination under the titles *Captain of the Host* and *Christ's Last Legion*, published in 1949; *By Faith Alone*, by Norval F. Pease, published in 1962; A. V. Olson's work, *Through Crisis to Victory*, published in 1966; and more recently *Movement of Destiny* by L. E. Froom, published in 1971. This is not to mention unpublished research papers produced by our theological seminary. Then there are various papers, tracts, journals, or books published independently of the church by individuals both within or on the fringes of the church, as it were, which deal frequently with the issue of this chapter and of this book.

From a historical perspective each of these sources addresses itself in greater or lesser measure directly or indirectly to the questions on salvation raised at and by the previously referred to General Conference of 1888. There the primary question was whether man is saved by faith in the righteousness which Jesus Christ alone worked out in His life here on earth and made available to man through Christ's crucifixion, death, and resurrection; or whether, in some way, man's obedience to the commandments of God is either an additional or the major requirement and means to salvation in the individual's experience.

The recent formal appeals of church leaders to the Adventist Church at large (referred to just above) have, without our sitting in judgment on previous generations, come as close as possible to acknowledging that the church in and around 1888 did not enter either as fully or as wholeheartedly into an experience in righteousness by faith, and particularly justification by faith, as was urged upon the church by several speakers at that epochal conference. These recent appeals have gone on to implore the church of today (to some extent collectively but particularly as individual members) to put aside all thought of self-righteousness, or justification to any degree by works of righteousness, and to rest salvation solely upon the means provided by Jesus Christ whereby to have His righteousness counted or attributed to the believer for righteousness because of or by means of faith in Him.

These recent appeals by church leadership, however, have not stopped at that point. The appeals have insisted that the acceptance by faith of the righteousness that Christ worked out nearly two thousand years ago in our behalf as the means of our justification must be followed, and will be followed, by the receiving of that same righteousness of Christ through the ministry of the indwelling Holy Spirit in the individual heart. By this means the individual will be growing in grace and the knowledge of God (a transformation of character, a com-

ing more and more completely to reflect Christ's likeness and image)—experiencing the accompanying and
consequent experience of sanctification that goes on in
the believer's life when once he has accepted and continues to accept Christ's justifying righteousness. It has
been implied, if not boldly stated, that to fail to enter
into this continuing and ongoing daily experience of
sanctification is to forfeit the covering righteousness of
Christ which He put to the individual's credit by the act
of justification, in which contract the righteousness of
Christ is *counted* to the individual as opposed to the
process of being *imparted* to him.

Perhaps the matter could be simplified even further
by contrasting, on the one hand, the righteousness that
Christ worked out nearly two thousand years ago
(which is now counted to the believer for righteousness
because of the believer's faith in Jesus Christ's life and
death and resurrection) with, on the other hand, any
necessity (in addition to that justifying righteousness)
for a work of Christ in the believer's heart here and now
before the assurance of salvation in Christ can be
claimed by the believer.

Now it seems evident that, unless we wish to assume
that those Christians who are living when Jesus Christ
comes the second time will be saved *on different terms*
from those of any previous generation that ever lived on
the earth, it should be possible to go to the Scriptures
and find the way of eternal life consistently illustrated,
demonstrated, and taught. This is not to deny for a
moment the possibility that the final generation of believers will have had and will continue to have an experience that is unique to them in certain respects, if
only because of what they are called upon to pass
through at the climax of the controversy between Christ

and Satan on this earth. But to suggest that they are saved on *different terms* seems to present a whole series of problems regarding God's dealings with man and the plan of salvation as presented in the Scriptures.

So may we take a look at the biblical presentation of what a man must do to be saved in God's eternal kingdom of righteousness. And as we move back to New Testament times, we might pause on our way to notice that Wesley and Calvin and Luther shared a clear understanding of the truth that no man can be saved by works of righteousness which he does, that his only hope of salvation is in the righteousness of Jesus Christ counted to him by faith, and that this justifying righteousness puts that man at peace with God and assures him of salvation to eternal life in Jesus Christ.

It is true that these three great Reformers held some rather vital differences on other aspects of the plan of salvation, but on this great central truth of justification by faith they were united. In fact, Wesley himself attributed his conversion (some might wish to call it a reconversion) to the reading of the preface to Luther's *Epistle to the Romans.*

We go back to the closing days of the first century and find John the beloved on the Isle of Patmos, isolated for his faith, and there receiving from God the "revelation of Jesus Christ." And repeatedly throughout the book he portrays the Saviour as man's substitute and surety, the one who has taken man's place and replaced man's failure with Christ's own victory. So we hear him addressing a paean of praise "to him who loves us and has freed us from our sins by his blood, and has made us to be a kingdom and priests to serve his God and Father—to him be glory and power for ever and ever! Amen." Revelation 1:5, 6, N.I.V.

Christ is the one "who is holy and true, who holds the key of David. What he opens, no one can shut; and what he shuts, no one can open." Revelation 3:7, N.I.V.

To the Laodiceans who do not realize their wretched and miserable naked condition spiritually, He offers Himself. "Here I am! I stand at the door and knock. If anyone hears my voice and opens the door, I will go in and eat with him, and he with me." Revelation 3:20, N.I.V. Christ is the heavenly merchantman. He stands at the door of the heart having in His hands everything that in turn is necessary to meet the shameful sinner's need. There is no other source, no substitute, no assistance that the sinner can give. He must acknowledge his need and choose to open the door. This act of opening the door, which the sinner alone can fulfill, is the one limitation the Saviour imposes on Himself and His gift. He forces Himself upon no one. He breaks into no hearts. He will only be an invited and welcomed guest, to rule and to bless as the host permits.

In many of the subsequent scenes of Revelation John was shown the adequacy of Jesus Christ and the uniqueness of that adequacy for man's salvation. In the vision of the throne in heaven, as created beings ascribe worship to God, John beholds a sealed scroll that contains information vital to the plan of salvation. John seems to sense the necessity for this scroll to be opened and for its contents to be made known: "There was no one in heaven or on earth or under the earth able to open the scroll or to look inside it. I was in tears because no one was found who was worthy to open the scroll or to look inside it. But one of the elders said to me: 'Do not weep; for the Lion from the tribe of Judah, the Scion of David, has won the right to open the scroll and break its seven seals.'

"Then I saw . . . a Lamb with the marks of slaughter upon him. . . . And the Lamb went up and took the scroll from the right hand of the One who sat on the throne. . . . And they were singing a new song:

" 'Thou art worthy to take the scroll and to break its seals, for thou wast slain and by thy blood didst purchase for God men of every tribe and language, people and nation; thou hast made of them a royal house, to serve our God as priests; and they shall reign upon earth.' " Revelation 5:3-10, N.E.B. Here again is the repeated assurance that Christ is worthy and He alone, that He has done what is essential, what is necessary, for the salvation of man. So in the portrayal of the final triumph of the redeemed as they stand before the throne and in front of the Lamb, wearing white robes and holding palm branches in their hands as the symbols of victory, "they shouted together: 'Victory to our God who sits on the throne, and to the Lamb!' " Revelation 7:10, N.E.B. The very prayers of the saints must be mingled with the incense which heaven has provided. Revelation 8:4. Those who finally are ushered into the city of God are "those whose names are written in the Lamb's book of life." Revelation 21:17, N.I.V.

At the same time there are repeated promises in this book of Revelation for the overcomer—for those who overcome as Christ overcame. By what means do they become "overcomers"? Let us ask by what means Christ maintained Himself as an overcomer throughout His life here on this earth. It was by complete, total, and persistent dependence upon His Father's power and submission to His Father's will. He had laid aside His prerogatives as God in His battle with temptation and the evil one. He insisted that His words and works were not His own but were those given Him of the Father to speak and to perform. Therefore, there need be no confusion. One fact stands out clearly: Full salvation can be offered and has been offered through Christ alone. Another fact is no less certain: Those who receive and accept His salvation by depending upon Him for salvation (as He depended upon His Father for power over sin and temptation) overcome in His overcoming and they will, by His grace. Only such overcomers will be entitled to sit down with Him in His throne as He, by virtue of His overcoming, has sat down with the Father in His throne. In fact, in the messages to the seven churches in the early chapters of the Revelation, it is Christ who constantly offers to the churches what they need in order to be overcomers. But the anguish of decision, of choice, of surrender, of choosing His will was still theirs. (See Revelation 3:21.)

In the letters of Paul to the New Testament church the subject of justification by faith is more fully and more explicitly dealt with than in any other portion of the Sacred Word. Nevertheless it is important to read Paul against the background of the teachings of Jesus as recorded in the Gospels and also against the total background of God's Old Testament revelation. It is important, if only on the principle of the unity of the Bible, not to divorce the theology of Paul from the "good news" teaching of Jesus Christ. It is equally important never to interpret the apostle Paul so that he in any way teaches ideas contrary to what Christ had taught before him.

Notice how clearly Paul analyzes and diagnoses the problem of the Jewish people of his time, at the same time that he declares his devotion to their eternal interests: "Brothers, my heart's desire and prayer to God for the Israelites is that they may be saved. For I can testify about them that they are zealous for God, but their zeal is not based on knowledge. Since they disregarded the righteousness that comes from God and sought to establish their own, they did not submit to God's righteousness for everyone who believes." Romans 10:1-4, N.I.V.

The basic problem here is that Israel had attempted to establish their own righteousness by a self-appointed devotion to law (whether moral or ceremonial or other categories), thinking that through strict devotion to the externals, the letter of the law, they could bring themselves to a condition of righteousness. In making this attempt they were neglecting the very righteousness that comes from God, that is God's gift—a gift provided by God alone. To this righteousness man can make no explicit contribution; it is perfectly adequate in and of itself and needs no human embellishment. This righteousness provided by God they had neglected and had attempted to substitute for it their own means for developing righteousness. Had they followed the light which God had given them in His Word and which particularly had been revealed to them in Christ by His gospel, they would have recognized that Christ puts an end to any human scheme for developing righteousness for those who believe, regardless of who they are. (Such schemes are doomed in any case. There is sufficiency only in Christ.) And this is for "everyone."

Sense the anguish of the apostle for his own people: "For I could wish that I myself were cursed and cut off from Christ for the sake of my brothers, those of my own race, the people of Israel." Romans 9:3, 4, N.I.V. He proceeds to list some of the advantages which had been Israel's by virtue of being the chosen people of God, the children of Abraham, the people of the covenant: "Theirs is the adoption as sons; theirs the divine glory,

the covenants, the receiving of the law, the temple worship and the promises. Theirs are the patriarchs, and
from them is traced the human ancestry of Christ, who is
God over all, forever praised! Amen." Verses 4, 5, N.I.V.

In appealing to his own people, the apostle Paul
draws upon the example of Abraham, their forefather.
He argues that if Abraham had been justified by works,
he would have had something to boast about; but the
Scriptures, he insists, say: "Abraham believed God, and
it was credited to him as righteousness." Romans 4:3,
N.I.V. Quoting from Genesis 15:6, the apostle is making
distinction between a gift and an obligation. When a
man works, he earns wages. Earnings do not come to
him as a gift, but their payment fulfills the obligation
resting upon the hiring party to him to pay him just
wages. But in the area of salvation, righteousness is a
gift to the man who does not attempt to earn righteousness by his own good works but rather trusts God "who
justifies the wicked"—and for him "his faith is credited
as righteousness." (See verses 4, 5.)

The apostle sees the birth of Isaac as an enacted parable that teaches that man's impossibility is God's opportunity. That which is "contrary" to nature, God can
perform. Where man is helpless and hopeless, God has
the means to provide. It was past all natural law that the
aged Abraham and Sarah should have a son. Nevertheless they had a son, a son of promise. The analogy is
drawn further in that the child born as a result of their
own devisings, Ishmael by name, was not the child of
promise and did not bring the promised blessings. On
the contrary, the whole story of humanity from that day
forward to the present troubled age has been affected by
conflict between the children of Isaac and the children
of Ishmael.

In showing his faith in God's promises, Abraham (although he wavered for a time) brought glory to God, since ultimately "he did not waver through unbelief regarding the promise of God, but was strengthened in his faith . . . , being fully persuaded that God had power to do what he had promised. This is why 'it was credited to him as righteousness.' " Verses 20-22, N.I.V. That the apostle is doing more than recounting well-known Hebrew history is evident as he continues to say, "The words 'it was credited to him' were written not for him alone, but also for us, to whom God will credit righteousness—for us who believe in him who raised Jesus our Lord from the dead. He was delivered over to death for our sins and was raised to life for our justification." Verses 23-25, N.I.V.

As we analyze what the apostle said regarding Abraham's experience, we find it clear that Abraham acted out his faith in God's promises. He willed the fulfillment of God's promises to himself and Sarah and through them to their own posterity and through that posterity to the whole world. The role of Abraham and Sarah was that of cooperation with and submission to the will of God, the plan of God, the provision of God. But the provision itself was made by God. They performed their human part for the conception and birth of a child; but there was no reason, there was no prior evidence, to lead them to expect any result from their efforts. The result was strictly, especially, and uniquely the miracle of God. (In one sense the birth of any child may be thought of as a "miracle"; but in the case of the child of promise it was a miracle of an undisputed and entirely different category, because Abraham and Sarah, and Sarah in particular, were beyond the age and capacity for conceiving and bearing a child—so much so that Sarah laughed when the promise was given by the heavenly messenger.)

The apostle culminates this developing line of reasoning concerning the experience of Abraham with the ringing declaration "Therefore, since we have been justified through faith, we have peace with God through our Lord Jesus Christ, through whom we have gained access by faith into this grace in which we now stand. And we rejoice in the hope of the glory of God." Romans 5:1, 2, N.I.V. As Abraham believed God and it was credited to Him for righteousness, or as righteousness, so we—those to whom the apostle was writing directly and those for whom his words have been preserved—may be justified through faith in what Christ has done for us. This changes our relationship to God from that which our nature merits. "While we were still sinners, Christ died for us."

"Since we have now been justified by His blood, how much more shall we be saved from God's wrath through him! For if, when we were God's enemies, we were reconciled to him through the death of his Son, how much more, having been reconciled, shall we be saved through his life!" Romans 5:9, 10, N.I.V. Notice that we have been reconciled, we did not reconcile ourselves to God. We did not provide the means for that reconciliation. Mankind as a whole knew not the significance of what God was doing in Christ, either in His life, or in His death, or in His resurrection. But it was the carrying out of the plan conceived in the mind of God from before the foundation of the world. In anticipation of our rebellion, God provided the means whereby to reconcile us to Him if we would have the faith of an Abraham in God's promises. By nature we would, as a race and as individuals, be deserving of God's wrath. But Christ, by living our life perfectly and dying the second death for us, and by His resurrection from the dead, provided the full means for all desiring it to be reconciled to God—to be made at peace with Him, being delivered from His eternal wrath against sin. His wrath ultimately destroys sin, because His presence is to sin a consuming fire. (See Hebrews 12:29.)

Paul's position on the relationship between law and grace, likewise, is clear and unequivocal. Whether speaking of Jews or Gentiles, he makes the charge that they "alike are all under sin." He then proceeds to quote Psalm 14 saying,

> " 'There is no one righteous, not even one;
>   there is no one who understands,
>   no one who searches for God.
> All have turned away
>   and together become worthless.
> There is no one who does good,
>   not even one.' "
>
> Romans 3:10-12, N.I.V.

According to Paul "The whole world" is "accountable to God." Romans 3:19, N.I.V. Paul has shown that the pagans have a witness to God in the things of nature and the consequences of creation. The Jews have received great light and knowledge of God—of His laws, and the covenants regarding those laws—by their relationship to God as a chosen people. And God proceeds to declare, "Therefore no one will be declared righteous in his sight by observing the law; rather, through the law we become conscious of sin." Romans 3:20, N.I.V. The law can show man his sin, either for the first time or repeatedly and to increasing depths; but it is powerless to cleanse, purify, or save that man who sees himself mirrored in the law.

What solution is there, therefore, for this whole race of man—"the whole world"? What is the remedy for man's lost condition, under the condemnation of law—no matter how great or small their knowledge of the laws on which God's kingdom is founded and by which it operates? Paul has the solution and offers it with joy: "But now a righteousness from God, apart from law, has been made known, to which the Law and the Prophets testify. This righteousness from God comes through faith in Jesus Christ to all who believe. There is no difference, for all have sinned and fall short of the glory of God, and are justified freely by his grace through the redemption that came by Christ Jesus." Romans 3:21-24, N.I.V.

There it is then. The solution comes from God. It comes to all who believe through faith in Jesus Christ. It comes to Jew and Gentile alike. In this respect there is no advantage to any human being no matter when he lived, under what era, what government, what culture, what "dispensation"—there is no difference. How can God offer this gift-righteousness without jeopardizing the law which is both an expression of His own character and the foundation of His government? God presented Jesus Christ "as a sacrifice of atonement, through faith in his blood. He did this to demonstrate his justice, because in his forbearance he had left the sins committed beforehand unpunished—he did it to demonstrate his justice at the present time, so as to be just and the one who justifies the man who has faith in Jesus." Verses 25, 26, N.I.V.

Christ has made the all-sufficient provision by being treated as the believer in Him would deserve to be treated apart from Christ. He is revealed as taking our punishment. He took the separation from God which sin always ultimately demands; He suffered this separation both in Gethsemane and on Calvary as witnessed by His threefold plea in the garden to be excused from making the sacrifice or for some other way to be found to redeem man without this awful separation that was coming upon Him. And on Calvary itself there was wrung from His almost bewildered heart and mind the cry: "My God, my God, why hast thou forsaken me?"

That which Christ has done (in living our life in perfect righteousness and in dying our death and rising victor over death and the grave) has purchased the right for God to justify man—sinful man—and yet Himself be just in so doing. This is the glory of the gospel of Jesus Christ, but to protect against quick misunderstandings Paul asks, "Do we, then, nullify the law by this faith? Not at all! Rather, we uphold the law." Verse 31, N.I.V. We pause a moment on this last text to observe a tragedy. An innumerable host of Christian people have claimed and still claim their salvation through Jesus Christ—claim justification by faith in Him. But they have come to think themselves utterly disconnected from and unrelated to God's laws anymore because of and through the gospel. They can even sing, "Free from the law, oh happy condition," and can claim that any who so much as express a desire to be loyal to God's laws thus deny the gospel because they still honor God's laws. It would seem that if there were no other such law-honoring verse in all the Scriptures (than this one from the apostle Paul who is acclaimed as master-teacher of justification by faith), this one text surely should uphold the continued validity of God's law.

We will want to probe more deeply into the latter issue subsequently. We have merely mentioned it in this present context where we are discussing Paul's clear understanding of the relationship between grace and law. It may also be observed at this point that in some instances Paul may seem to be speaking more specifically of the moral law as opposed to the law of ceremonies and ordinances. However, his overall New Testament argument is that no human effort to obey God's law is adequate to provide any individual with a righteousness that will save him in God's kingdom. Such efforts to obey God's laws are wholly inadequate if only because they make no atonement for past transgressions. And who is there who would dare to claim that he is perfectly obedient at all times to every one of God's commandments—who beside Jesus Christ?

So grace does not destroy law, but neither does obedience to God's law in itself and of itself destroy grace. Only if the one rendering such obedience (even with the indwelling power of the Holy Spirit) wishes to present that obedience as the argument for his own salvation—wishes to argue that his obedience makes it just for God to justify him—is he disrupting grace. But, as we have seen, God can be just only when He justifies the man who has faith in Jesus Christ and who constantly and always recognizes that "His righteousness is mine."

In the Gospels the preaching and teaching of Jesus Christ Himself is presented regarding God's plan for making a man righteous and giving him a place in the eternal kingdom. Consider that text which above all others is regarded as the essence of the gospel—the essence of the good news of the kingdom which Christ came to open to mankind, Jew and Gentile alike. And what does it say? "For God so loved the world that he gave his one and only Son, that whoever believes in him shall not perish but have everlasting life." John 3:16, N.I.V. Isn't that clear enough? Isn't that straightforward enough? Whosoever *believes* in Him shall not perish but have everlasting life. Nothing is even said about works of righteousness; nothing is even said about law or laws. It is the bald and bold assurance that he who believes will have everlasting life.

It is easy to forget the context in which Christ's great gospel promise resides. It appears in the heart of His discourse to a one-man audience—Nicodemus, the highly educated, highly cultured, influential and powerful ruler in Israel. To this ruler who came to Jesus by night (presumably because he was not anxious to be identified in any way with this uneducated and new teacher in Israel) Christ gave the most complete statement He ever gave of the steps one must take from sin and despair to righteousness and eternal life, and this statement was made early in His ministry. What was the essence of this discourse? "You, Nicodemus, must be born again, born from above. A new life from outside yourself must come from God to you if you are to have eternal life. You cannot even *see* the kingdom of heaven unless you accept this bestowal, this gift, this endowment from outside and beyond yourself—from God who alone can provide it. There is no other way, Nicodemus, even for you, a teacher in Israel, one highly respected and honored for his upright way of life and for his high rank in Israel. The only hope for you is to be born again, born of God, born of the Holy Spirit."

Nicodemus wanted to get into the how of it. "How can these things be?" He was trying to fog the issue by acting as though Christ were speaking physically of his having to be born a second time from his mother, although the expression which Christ used was not unfamiliar to the

Jews. (They used it to speak of those who came from outside Israel as converts to the Jewish faith.) Jesus began to give Nicodemus some illustrations to help him understand.

"Nicodemus, you have no control of the wind. It comes and it goes. You cannot change its direction. You cannot diminish its force. You cannot even see it of itself, but you can see its effects. You can see the results of its action. Well, Nicodemus, neither can you control the means by which you can be saved in the eternal kingdom. It is not in your power or that of any man to control the work of the Holy Spirit. This is the work of God. This is God's gift to you. You cannot earn it, you cannot deserve it. You can accept or reject, and this alone can you do. And only you can do it."

Again Nicodemus persists in asking *"How* can this be? *How* can this be accomplished?" And Jesus moves him on to perhaps more familiar ground yet. "Do you remember, Nicodemus, what Moses did back in the wilderness when rebellious Israel was being destroyed by a plague of serpents? When Israel cried out for deliverance, do you remember how the Lord ordered a brass serpent to be cast and put up on a pole and then told the suffering people to *look* at that brass serpent? If they would look at it, they would live; but if they refused to look at it, they would die. Do you remember this, Nicodemus? Was there any power in that serpent, Nicodemus—power to heal, power to save the dying from swift death? Then what was it that effected the healing, the salvation of those who looked? It was the demonstration of their faith in the means which only God could provide—that brought them healing. Nicodemus, don't stop to ask for the rationale of My plan of salvation. Don't stop to try to calculate how much love or what kind of love God has for you that He would make such a provision. But accept it, Nicodemus. And someday I, the Son of man, will be lifted up just as the brass snake was lifted up in the wilderness, and all who have believed or will believe on me when I am so lifted up will have eternal life."

It is in this context, then, that the universally acclaimed words of John 3:16 were spoken.

Before we leave this chapter and our attempt to answer the question, "What must I do to be saved?" and before we leave the teachings of Jesus in the Gospels regarding the way of salvation, let us look at one or two other real-life situations in which Jesus was asked the question, "What shall I do to be saved?"

In the three synoptic Gospels—Matthew, Mark and Luke—we have accounts of a rich young ruler who came to Jesus, kneeling before Him in great earnestness and supplication after he had seen how Jesus dealt with a group of mothers with their children and infants who came seeking His blessing. Kneeling before the Lord, this rich young ruler asked, "Teacher, what good deed must I do, to have eternal life?" Matthew 19:16, R.S.V. (See Mark 10:17; Luke 18:18, R.S.V.) And Jesus questioned why the wealthy young ruler had looked to Him as one who could answer this question. "One there is who is good," Jesus said to him. "If you would enter life, keep the commandments." Matthew 19:17, R.S.V. Immediately, referring to the commandments, the young man eagerly asked, "Which?" It is significant that Jesus began to quote to him some of the second table of the Ten Commandments, those dealing with man's relationship to man: "You shall not kill, You shall not commit adultery, You shall not steal, You shall not bear false witness, Honor your father and mother and, You shall love your neighbor as yourself." Verses 18, 19, R.S.V.

With unabated eagerness the young man assured the Lord that "all these I have observed; what do I still lack?" Verse 20, R.S.V. And then it was that the Lord who will one day be judge of the souls of all men put His finger, as it were, upon the plague spot in the young man's character. In spite of the fact that he was outwardly an upright and noble young man, one whom Jesus particularly loved as He looked upon him, Jesus brought him to the test of his soul when He said, "If you would be perfect, go, sell what you possess and give to the poor, and you will have treasure in heaven; and come, follow me." Verse 21, R.S.V.

We need to look very carefully at this account because on the surface it looks as though Christ is teaching salvation by works, thus presenting a legalistic basis for salvation. He quotes from the Ten Commandments to indicate the things which the young man should do in order to have eternal life. Could it be that Christ here teaches salvation by works of righteousness that we have done and that His servant Paul would insist later that our salvation is not based upon works of righteousness which we have done or can do? Could there be a contradiction here between the Lord and His chosen apostle?

The scriptural record tells us that when the young man heard the conditions which Christ was laying down, he went away sorrowful. Why should he go away sorrowful if he actually had been keeping the commandments, even from his youth upward? Why should he be distressed when Christ had indicated that obedience to the commandments is the basis for eternal life? There obviously was something lacking in the kind or quality of obedience rendered by this rich young ruler so that when that specific lack was pointed up, he found himself unwilling to meet the terms laid down by the Lord and so in sorrow turned away from the Saviour.

We may ask where faith and surrender come into the young man's experience. He was drawn to Jesus. He saw the godliness of Christ's manner, attitude, and actions (even toward women and children who normally did not command the center stage in those days). He saw Christ's disciples giving the women and children the typical and expected treatment that they would have received in approaching an important person, a public person, a leader. Then he heard Christ rebuking His disciples for treating these human beings in this way, he saw Him inviting them to come to Him, to be blessed by Him, to be comforted by Him, to be reassured by Him, to have their burdens lifted by Him. The rich young ruler recognized in the ways of Jesus Christ a power and a quality to which he himself was a stranger—a power that drew him to Christ as to a magnet. What then was missing? What then was lacking in the young ruler's experience?

The young ruler must have displayed outward conformity to the laws of God. He was undoubtedly most sincere when protesting that he had kept the commandments. So much so that he wanted to know what else he lacked, or what he lacked yet—for he sensed no lack in the consistency of his obedience to the commandments. He probably was an upright, highly esteemed, well-to-do young man in his community. He was a leader—possibly a religious leader of the people. People would have called him a good man, an upright young man, certainly a moral man. But when Jesus put His finger on the root of selfishness that was growing in the depth of this young man's heart, a terrible decision had to be faced by the rich young ruler. Christ was calling not only for a favorable reaction to Him but rather for a surrender of the specific idols that had really occupied the throne room of the ruler's heart. He was asking for a commitment that would be demonstrated by complete dependence upon Christ and unreserved submission to His will, for the young ruler would have to give up his riches, distribute them to the poor, and then follow Christ. He would then be without any assurance of support for the life-style that he had known, presumably, from his birth until the present time in his life.

The rich young ruler was being called upon to demonstrate complete faith in Christ—not just the kind of faith that would acknowledge Christ's divinity or His Messiahship but a faith of commitment, a faith of trust, a faith that would involve things, realities. This young man needed faith that would say, "Lord, I am putting myself completely in Your hands. I trust You completely. I believe in You with all my heart and mind and spirit. I will go anywhere You want me to go and do anything You want me to do. Nothing shall stand between my soul and You; not one piece of the wealth that is mine shall be held back."

It seems clear that in the experience of the rich young ruler we have a call for conversion in which the terms "faith" or "surrender" or "justification" never once appear. The surface of the case would even suggest that formal obedience to the Ten Commandments would entitle a person to eternal life. So the question put to Jesus by the young ruler was couched in such terms. But when we look beneath the surface, when we look at what Christ was really asking this young man to do, we see indeed that he was being asked to show his faith by works—not formal, routine, crossless works but works of obedience to the commandments of God that would cost him everything he had. We do not know whether the Lord would have restored to him his riches as he once restored the wealth of Job in Old Testament times, or whether upon evidence that the young man was ready to act in obedience the Lord would have said to him as once He said to Abraham, "Now I know that you would be willing to obey at any cost, but I have made provision so that you don't have to go through with the sacrifice."

The fact remains that the young man was presented with the test of the reality and quality of his obedience—whether it was an obedience of love or an obedience of self-righteousness and self-justification. Apparently the young man lacked the obedience of love. For when shown how to demonstrate love for God supremely by demonstrating love to his fellowmen, immediately the ruler could not pass the test. He was not prepared to pay the price. He could not bring himself to cast his will, his all, upon Jesus, trusting Him to supply what hitherto had been provided by his wealth. Instead, he went away. And he grieved over his failure.

Another individual, a lawyer, came to Jesus with practically the same question. Doubtless he had been trained in Jewish law, perhaps both ecclesiastical and secular, but possibly more ecclesiastical than secular. And he puts Jesus to the test, saying, "Teacher, what shall I do to inherit eternal life?" Luke 10:25, R.S.V. In this instance, Jesus asks him what is written in the law—"how do you read?" Very appropriate questions to ask of the lawyer. If anyone should know what was written in the law, he should. And he did. He did not give a superficial answer. He gave an answer of great discernment: "You shall love the Lord your God with all your heart, and with all your soul, and with all your strength, and with all your mind; and your neighbor as yourself." Verse 27, R.S.V. And Jesus says to the lawyer, "You have answered right; do this, and you will live." Verse 28, R.S.V.

Once again it looks as though Jesus is teaching salvation by works, by obedience to the laws of God. But if we will note, the lawyer did not cite individual laws out of the Ten Commandments, but cited rather the summary, the underlying principle of the Ten Commandments, which makes obedience to the first four commandments an expression of supreme love to God and obedience to the latter six commandments an expression of love to one's fellowman. So love is shown to be the heart of the law of God. One could even suspect that "the law" in this case was a reference to more than the Ten Commandments. In reality the entire Old Testament is an elaboration upon and an expression of the laws of God, particularly enunciated in the Ten Commandments. The lawyer most likely quoted Deuteronomy 6:5 for demanding one's supreme allegiance to God, and Leviticus 19:18 for one's obligation to his neighbor. So he did not quote directly from the Ten Commandments, although the two principles which he enunciated are elsewhere used by Christ as the summary of the Ten Commandments.

So we have here, in a little different way, the principle that love is the fulfilling of the law of God, a principle later enunciated by the apostle Paul. (See Romans 13:10.)

Now it is well known to all readers of the New Testament that within this dialogue with the lawyer, Jesus told the parable of the Good Samaritan in response to the lawyer's effort to justify himself by raising the issue of who was his neighbor. In other words, the lawyer recognized the soundness of the biblical principles and the correctness of Christ's statement that if he would indeed fulfill the entire law of God, he could have eternal life. But somewhere in recognizing his inadequacy and acknowledging his virtual unwillingness to carry out the total commitment called for by the conditions, he tried to evade the issue by raising the question as to who his neighbor really was.

It helps explain things a bit to recognize that this was a matter of continual discussion among Jewish lawyers and teachers because for one reason and another a type of exclusiveness had become characteristic of the religious experience of God's chosen people. As a result, they were willing to recognize certain people as their neighbors and would disregard certain other people entirely. Among those who would never be recognized as neighbors were the people from whom Christ drew an example in His story of the Good Samaritan. This Samaritan, whom the Jews would never recognize as a neighbor, acted the part of a true neighbor to a Jew. In other words, he demonstrated par excellence the golden rule. He did for someone what he knew that someone would never, never do for him in similar circumstances, and in so doing he exemplified the character of God. He reflected what Jesus Christ Himself had actually come to do and was even then doing by His life here on earth. Christ was placing Himself in jeopardy at infinite cost to Himself for the benefit of those who in general would never reciprocate His love and thoughtfulness.

In the story the lawyer is finally called upon by Christ to tell Him which of the three men who walked down the road to Jericho from Jerusalem was really neighbor to the poor wretch who was robbed and thrown in the ditch for dead. A priest had passed him by, and a Levite had looked at him and passed him by. A Samaritan came, saw him, had pity on him, went to him, and treated him. Then the Samaritan used his own beast to take the injured man to an inn. There the Samaritan took care of the wounded man. As the Samaritan left the inn the next day, he gave the innkeeper money to care for this man. "If it costs you more than this," the Samaritan told the innkeeper, "I will reimburse you when I return this way." In great reluctance, the lawyer admitted which of the three was neighbor to him who fell among robbers. But even then he could not bring himself to take the name of a Samaritan on his lips. Instead he said, "The one who showed mercy on him." Luke 10:36, R.S.V. But his answer was adequate for Jesus to be able to take it and say to him, "Go and do likewise."

Again we are confronted with a question: Was Jesus here teaching salvation by works? On the surface it might look that way. But if we would think the matter through, we would see that we have a parallel here to the experience of the rich young ruler described earlier. Again it is not a superficial obedience, not a technical obedience to God's will, that is called for. It is an identification with the character and spirit of God. It is an alignment of one's self with the purposes and ways of God, not only in His character as the ruler of the universe but in His dealings with men, the people of His creation. It is a self-sacrificing commitment that is illustrated in the story of the Good Samaritan. It is heart religion that Christ was eliciting in His response to the lawyer's inquiry, and it is heart religion alone that will put us in touch with heaven and make heaven a place where we will be happy eternally, world without end.

In both these instances, that of the rich young ruler on the one hand and that of the lawyer on the other, they were not lacking in formal knowledge of truth. They were not ignorant of the Bible as the Word of God, but neither of them had ever let the principles of the teachings of the Word penetrate the inner citadel of the heart. They may have been generous with the temple of the Lord, casting their shekels into the treasury, as in the story about the widow who gave her two mites. They may both have been men of exemplary external character and who gave technical obedience to the requirements of God's laws. But they had not allowed themselves to be confronted with the all-consuming reality of the demands of the law of God; neither had they faced their own inability to render acceptable obedience to those laws—the kind of obedience that would make it safe for such a person to be admitted to the heavenly courts without prospect of a new rebellion such as that which began in heaven and was extended to Eden.

Had these men truly attempted to carry out the instructions of Christ to the degree and extent that He asked of them, they would soon have been forced to acknowledge their own inability to render that type of obedience, then they would have been in the frame of mind to accept the obedience rendered in their behalf (and in the behalf of each of us) by Him who came down from heaven to do His Father's will perfectly. Even then, He was moving toward Calvary to pay the price that sinners ought to pay, in order that His perfect obedience might be counted to them for righteousness and that their broken hearts might be opened to the indwelling of His promised Spirit. The Spirit, in turn, would bring the presence and the character of God the Father and God the Son into the life indwelt by the Spirit of God. So these two illustrations closely parallel what God attempted to teach Israel of old by requiring of them an obedience which they of themselves were incapable of rendering. God demanded this kind of obedience of them so that they might come to recognize the fallen nature which they had both inherited and cultivated. Also He wanted them to recognize their utter dependence on a Substitute represented before them daily in the sacrificial services of the temple. They needed to see that the blood of the substitute Lamb was accepted before God for the forgiveness and cleansing of sin even as the sacrificial blood made it possible for the penitent worshiper to approach without condemnation the law of God that was secured in the Most Holy place of the sanctuary. The obedience of Another would stand in his place, and the punishment of Another would make it possible for him to go free from condemnation before the law of God.

In reality, the requirement of obedience which Jesus presented to the rich young ruler and to the lawyer is what God's law has always demanded and always will demand, but it is an obedience which man himself cannot render. Hence his need of the gospel of Christ as his Substitute and Surety through which he becomes acceptable to God and a dwelling place for the Spirit of God who will live out the life of God in every submissive and God-believing sinner.

It is important, in evaluating the response given by Jesus Christ to the inquiry of the rich young ruler and of the lawyer, to note that Jesus was primarily answering the question, What? He was not directly answering the question, How? In other words, the plan of salvation, to be effective by restoring what was lost in Eden, must renew in those citizens who will be entrusted with eternal life a capacity for and a choosing of a life of obedience to the will of God, whether formally expressed in commandments and laws (such as the Ten Commandments) or in specific instruction to individuals under varying circumstances. The law of God, which is virtually a writing out of God's own character, cannot possibly be modified in any way or laid to one side in order to accommodate the sinful nature and actions of man. For God to deny His holy law would virtually be to speak against His own character. So the plan of salvation, to be effective, must restore man to harmony with the law of God, the law of love as we have seen it—supreme love to God and unequivocal love to fellowman. Really this is what Christ is stressing in His answers to these two men.

Now subsequently, having laid down the conditions for meeting God's requirements, the Lord leads on in each case to show what must underlie an agreement to obey the moral law of God if it is to be more than a lip service to the required standard and conditions of eternal life. In the illustration of the Good Samaritan the Lord showed the utter selflessness of the one who represented the character of God in the story, and the complete provision made to meet the need of the victim who fell among thieves. (The victim represents any human being fallen under the power of the devil whom Christ described as a liar and a murderer from the beginning.)

The victim of the robbery, in the story, was utterly helpless to cope with his own situation. Left unattended he would have died. The one who takes compassion on him and thus shows himself to be a real neighbor makes complete provision to meet the needs of the beaten victim, even future need until restoration should be complete. For those who had ears to hear it and faith to receive it, this certainly was a demonstration of how completely a man needs help from above, from outside himself, if he is to escape the pit of sin and the power of Satan. And it was and is this spirit of utter selflessness demonstrated by the Good Samaritan that must be seen in the life of one who claims to love God supremely and his neighbor as himself. A demonstration of partiality for those closer to him by ties of blood or belief could not be enough. To be a true reflection of the character of God, the kindness and thoughtfulness shown must be strictly impartial and must leap over those barriers that divide humanity into warring and hating segments. But how a human being was to acquire these characteristics of godlikeness the lawyer seemed neither to ask nor to want to know.

By His illustration of the Good Samaritan, Christ showed the lawyer a picture of what one who truly keeps God's commandments is like. Indeed he is like God, he is like Christ. His religion is not fearing. His religion is life-transforming, life-changing, and utterly selfless. Had the lawyer desired it and had he asked for it as Nicodemus before him, the Lord could and surely would have answered the question as to how he could go and do what the Good Samaritan had done—how he could go and be like the Christ to whom he had been so attracted.

As far as the rich young ruler is concerned, he was not only told the general standard that he must meet in order to be saved but was shown specifically those aspects of his life and experience that were shutting him off from oneness with God in character, in purpose, and in performance. And had he wished deliverance from the power of the wealth which he worshiped, he could have been given it as readily as was Zacchaeus or

Matthew the publican. But the tragic account is that he went away sorrowful, for he had great riches. He did not wait to discover the *how;* because, when he saw the real nature of the *what* (which he had confidently thought he already had performed), he was not prepared to pay the price no matter who would help him to discover the *how* of it all.

And so it may be today that when we ask, What must I do to be saved? We need to be in dead earnest and completely sincere in asking the question. When the answer comes as to what standard we must reach (and when we are given true-to-life examples of that standard), we must be ready to go on and ask, "Lord, how can this become true for me? How shall I relate myself to You and to my fellowmen so that this ideal of likeness to God shall become a reality in my daily living?"

May we now say that we have by no means exhausted the teachings of Jesus on this vital question, What must I do to be saved? Neither have we recounted by any means all of the illustrations regarding it that could be drawn from Christ's life and ministry. But in other connections and in other contexts we will have occasion to come back again to the Lord's answers to the supreme question that can ever be asked by a sinful human being. And perhaps that last category includes every one of us.

3. The Heart Tug of God's Love

The entire mission and message of Christ during His life here on this earth had a multiple purpose which nevertheless was all of one. He came to reveal God, to show men what God is truly like, to give them the most complete revelation in a living person of what God is like that man has ever received. In addition to revealing to man what God is like, He came to draw men to God.

Christ, in showing us what God is like, set a perfect example; for although He was "God with us," yet He Himself was also man. And in His revelation to us of God, in His victory over sin and death and the devil, He made Himself as dependent upon His Father as man is dependent upon God for godlikeness. He also, however, came to create for us a way back to God, a way for us who had by our sins shut ourselves off from direct access to God. And in order to provide us with this way, He not only was our perfect Example but also our Redeemer. He showed us what God is like, what we can be like when we are truly like God; paid the penalty for our rebellion against God; bridged our separation from Him by dying our death as He had lived our life; and thus He can offer us, on the basis of the most glorious exchange ever offered to mankind, the way back to God. He made us

51

52

acceptable again to God in Himself. (See John 14:1-11.)

To know how acceptable we can be to God, we should ask the Scriptures to show us how acceptable Jesus Christ was to God. In making us acceptable again to God, Christ became our Example, our Redeemer, and our Substitute and Surety. He took our case, He took upon Himself our cause. He picked us up out of our depths of sin, degradation, and rebellion. He battled every principle of temptation to which mankind can be subject, and He endured those trials and temptations to a depth fathomed by no other person before Him or after Him. By this means He came through more than conqueror. He has somewhat to give to us who have nothing in ourselves to bring to God but our heritage of sin and our own practice of it. (See Hebrews 8:1-6.)

All of this was latent within Christ's words to Nicodemus (to which we referred in the previous chapter) when He said, "As Moses lifted up the serpent in the wilderness, so must the Son of man be lifted up, that whoever believes in him may have eternal life." John 3:14, 15, R.S.V. We can believe that Jesus, as He spoke to Nicodemus in that night retreat, looked forward some three years to Calvary and knew that the revelation of God's love given there would have a power to draw men to God that would be incomparable with any other power in heaven or on earth.

From time to time during His ministry Jesus came back to this theme of His being lifted up. On one occasion as He was disputing with the Jews about His mission and their unbelief of Him and His mission, He said, "When you have lifted up the Son of man, then you will know that I am he, and that I do nothing on my own authority but speak thus as the Father taught me." John 8:28, R.S.V. When a group of Greeks sought Jesus out at one of the annual feasts in Jerusalem, He saw in these aliens a firstfruits of the harvest from every nation, kindred, tongue, and people that would ultimately come to a knowledge of Him and the eternal life which He offers. And although an overwhelming sense in anticipation of the cross pressed in upon Him, He said, "Now is the judgment of this world, now shall the ruler of this world be cast out; and I, when I am lifted up from the earth, will draw all men to myself." In explanation of the significance of His words, John continues by saying, "He said this to show by what death he was to die." John 12:32, 33, R.S.V.

What would it be about the crucifixion of this Man that would have the power to draw men to God? Death by crucifixion was one of the weapons of Roman power and at times was ruthlessly carried out upon many victims at the same time and place so that the crosses might remind one of a forest of trees. But this cross and this Victim were unique. In what ways and why?

The cross of Jesus Christ at Calvary was not the beginning of His mission to draw men unto Himself but, from an earthly point of view, the end, the climax. In reality He had been dying our death every day that He lived our life—from the standpoint that He endured every day a conflict with evil, with the power of Satan, either directly or through other evil spirits or through evil men. This conflict tore His heart in a way that we can never experience and can never understand. He who had lived throughout eternity in the atmosphere of heaven, in the companionship of the Godhead, was met at every hand by the results of the work of the rebel who was a liar and a murderer from the beginning of his rebellion against God—Lucifer, that one time lightbearer in the presence of God. (See John 8:44; Isaiah 14:12-14.)

54

Calvary in one sense was a lesser Gethsemane. That is, the decision to go through to Calvary was made in Gethsemane. There "beneath the old olive trees" Jesus Christ wrestled with the question as to whether or not He would finally complete His mission as our Substitute and Surety and Redeemer by permitting Himself to pass under the shadow of death for our sins. In Gethsemane the symbolic cup of His final trial—the separation from His Father for the first time in all eternity—trembled in His hand. There He pleaded three times with the Father to provide some other way of escape for sinful man without His drinking that indescribably bitter cup. (See Mark 14:32-42.)

To place Himself even for a time and even in a special way and degree under the power of him who claimed all the dead as his prisoners—his perpetual and permanent prisoners—was an anguished decision the like of which we can never know. It reminds us of the temptations of our Lord in the wilderness early in His ministry. During that experience the devil had the audacity to convey Christ first to a pinnacle of the temple and then to the top of a high mountain. (See Matthew 4:1-11.) That Christ permitted Himself to be thus temporarily in the hands as it were of the master craftsman of evil and rebellion against the government of God is almost incomprehensible. Perhaps this is why it has been said that the cross of Calvary is only a glimpse to our dull human senses of the anguish and the pain that has been in the heart of God since sin made its awful debut in heaven itself in the rebellion of Lucifer and those among the angelic host who were deceived by him.

In Gethsemane Christ clung to the ground as one beaten by a desperate storm, as though the ground could save Him from the awful abyss of separation from His

Father that loomed immediately ahead of Him, just hours away. In Gethsemane He fell to the ground faint and dying, and an angel messenger came to strengthen and sustain Him physically for the battle to which His will and choice had committed Him. It could very well be that our Lord would have become our sacrifice in Gethsemane had not the angel strengthened Him to endure an awful night and a seemingly endless day before He died on the cross. (See Luke 22:36-46.)

That He could have delivered Himself from the anguish of Gethsemane was demonstrated by the inability of the temple rabble and mob to take Him prisoner until He released His angel guardian and permitted Himself to be taken and bound; and even in the binding, He loosed His hands to heal one wounded by an awkward sword-swinging fisherman named Peter and then permitted Himself to be bound and led away to be mocked and beaten in a complete devastation of all human justice and in a complete mockery of the laws of the land in which He lived. (See Luke 22:47-51.)

Follow Jesus through the series of illegal trials convened at night on short notice, with false witnesses presenting false accusations readily received by false judges who could not wait to condemn Him to death and who were prepared to threaten, cajole, and bribe the Roman governor to give a guilty verdict against his better judgment, though himself no saint. Follow the account through the Gospels. They devote a greater proportion of their pages to the final events and to the death of Jesus than to His ministry. Then remember it was not the Romans who put Him to death, it was not the cross that killed Him, it was not the priests alone who condemned Him to death; it was my sins and it was your sins. It was we who nailed Him there, along with all who have ever been a part of the web of humanity, whether Gentile or Jew, Roman or barbarian.

If in prayerful and earnest contemplation of what Christ did in coming to be our Redeemer, our Substitute and our Surety, we are not drawn to God in Him, then no other power in heaven or on earth can move us toward God. In His case it was not the nails through His hands that killed Him, not the awful weight of His sagging body, emaciated by hunger and thirst, not the belittling jeers of the mob surrounding the cross, or the curses of the two malefactors, crucified one on each side of Him—not one or all of these things together took the life of the Son of God. It was rather that which set Him dying in Gethsemane, that which cast a cloud of gloom over Him at the Jerusalem temple when the Greeks came seeking Him—it was altogether and only the separation between Himself and His Father, brought about by His voluntary assumption of our sins. This separation led to His death in just a very few hours, when normally victims lingered on the cross for days and it was difficult to tell just when life left the smitten human forms.

When Christ died, He died victorious, He died in triumph, He died a conqueror over sin, death, and the devil. The ultimate end of sin was assured. The end of death was assured by His death. But He could have failed. He could have faltered. He could have sinned. He was not a make-believe example or a make-believe substitute, or a make-believe surety for us. "After this Jesus, knowing that all was now finished, said (to fulfill the scripture), 'I thirst.' A bowlful of vinegar stood there; so they put a sponge full of the vinegar on hyssop and held it to his mouth. When Jesus had received the vinegar, he said, 'It is finished'; and he bowed his head and gave up his spirit." John 19:28-30, R.S.V.

Even when Christ was being taunted by the rulers of the people as He hung in anguish and agony upon the cross, what would it have meant to you and me if He had come down from the cross as His tormentors bade Him to do?

WHAT IF HE HAD COME DOWN?

"LET HIM COME DOWN!"

The challange was flung into the teeth of the Galilean by
                                        cultured
voices that were now disdainful, mocking, bitter.
The owners of the voices felt that they had their man
                                        just where they wanted Him . . .

        on a cross
      nailed there by spikes through His hands and
                        through His feet,
      lifted up above the earth,
        in full sight of men,
            beneath the light of noontide sun.
Perhaps others would learn from His fate,
                learn that it did not pay to speak out against the
authority of those who sat "in Moses' seat."

"LET HIM COME DOWN!"

He may have worsted them in the bitter debates in which
                                they had sought to humble Him,
      may have eluded the double-pronged dilemmas upon which
                                they had hoped to spike Him,
          but where was His debating prowess now?
        Where were those miracles to prove His
                                connection with God?
          Where the multitudes that had thronged His steps?
          Where those loyal disciples?
And, just incidentally, where was that heavenly Father
                        of His now?
The questions were accompanied by derisive laughter,
      in which these men who stood in holy office,
                    who wore the vestments of Aaron,
        who served as intermediaries between the people
                        and their God, . . .

these men tried to outdo one another in showing
their hatred,
their venom,
and their spite.
All this was implicit in their challenge:
"LET HIM COME DOWN!"

It was true that He had escaped the mob intent on murdering
Him at Nazareth,
had "passed through the midst" when they
would have
taken Him in the Temple,
had held spellbound the officers sent out to
take Him captive,
but they had Him now. "Let Him come down now!"

They reminded one another of His many pretentious
claims, and as His now-battered
body sagged and writhed on the
gibbet, they would cast some re-
minders up at Him:
"I say! Thou that destroyest the Temple and buildest
it in
three days, save Thyself!"
"Oh, yes. If Thou be the Son of God,
come down from the cross."
"Dost not Thou remember, Thou art the Son of God?"
"Great Healer!"—"Great Resurrection Man—
look at Your sagging head,
Your bloody beard,
Your puny arms.
Save Thyself! Heal Thyself!"
"He saved others, Himself He cannot save."
A newcomer read the inscription above His head: "King of
the Jews,"
and a new tirade developed:
"Supposed to be the King of Israel. . . . Ha!
Well, if He be the King of Israel,
let Him now come down from the cross,
and we will believe Him, won't we!"

"Let God deliver Thee now, if He will have Thee.
  We're all ready;
    we're waiting;
      we're watching;
        we're all here."

BUT WHAT IF HE HAD COME DOWN!
    had released His hands from the cruel spikes,
      had then released His feet,
        had wiped away the blood sweat from His brow and
had jumped nimbly down from the cross.
    had stood there before them in a blaze of glory,
              confronting
           His cruel tormentors?

What if He *had* come down?
Would those vaunted priests and rabbis have fled in terror,
              pale with fear,
      pushing and jostling one another
  lest He catch up with the hindermost of them?
Or would they have descended upon their prey like a pack of
  wild, ravenous dogs, with their quarry at bay,
    ready to tear Him limb from limb?

What does it matter?
    HE DID NOT COME DOWN.

Perhaps He could not.
    Perhaps that was one thing too difficult for Him—
         one miracle even He could not perform.
Was that possible?
Had He not restored a completely severed ear to its
              rightful place on a man's head?
  Had He not called to life a man whose body was already rotting?
  Had He not restored sight to blind eyes?
    Had He not replaced the rotted fingers, toes, and noses
     of the tragic victims of the dreaded leprosy?
    Had He not rehabilitated maniacs with a word?
Could He not then have come down from the cross?
Yes, of course He could—a thousand times yes!

If death and the grave could not hold Him when He was dead,
    could He not have resisted them when alive?
Could not He who released His hands from the mob in
                the garden
    have released those same hands from the soldiers at
                the cross?
And would not twelve legions of angels have come to His
                aid, if called?
CERTAINLY, HE COULD HAVE COME DOWN FROM THE CROSS.

AND YET, HE *COULDN'T* COME DOWN FROM THE CROSS.
What if He *had* come down?
  What if He had responded to the challenge of the
                scribes and rulers?
Oh, Jesus Christ had the power to come down from that cross,
    but He was held there,
        held by a force which He could neither deny nor gainsay.

It wasn't the coarse spikes through His feet,
    nor the jagged spikes through His hands, that held
                Him there.
It wasn't fear of the Roman guard,
        nor fear of the spineless Roman governor, Pilate,
              that held Him there.
Only one thing held Him there,
  and that one thing was His eternal love for man.
HE COULD NOT COME DOWN FROM THE CROSS AND
        REMAIN TRUE TO HIMSELF,
    could not come down and yet show that love leads to
    the absolute and complete surrender of self to the
              service of others.
He could not come down and yet show that God so loved the world
  that He gave His only-begotten Son to die for it.
He could not come down and yet demonstrate that as the
              eternal Son of God He had power
              to lay down His life
    and power to take it up again.
He could not come down from the cross and still fulfill
              the word of John the Baptist:
    "Behold the Lamb of God."

Yes, that was it—"the Lamb of God, which taketh away the
sin of the world"—
the Lamb that in the plan of God had been
"slain from the foundation of the world."

He could not come down without violating the promise made
to Adam and Eve in Eden: the seed of the woman was to bruise the
head of the serpent;
could not come down and still be the fulfillment of all the
lambs
and kids
and goats
that had been slain since Eden, in the sacrifices—
sacrifices that were to be to man
a perpetual reminder of his sin
and a penitential acknowledgment of it;
could not have come down without denying that by the shedding
of blood—the blood of the Lamb—there would be
remission, or forgiveness, of sin.

HE COULD NOT COME DOWN FROM THE CROSS.
To hang on the cross,
to die on the cross, was to carry to completion the
mysterious
purpose of Christ's declaration from the throne of God:
"A body hast thou prepared me. . . .
Lo, I come . . . to do thy will, O God."
When the mocking priests declared, "He saved others;
himself he cannot save,"
they unwittingly declared a profound truth.
It was true, so true.
He could not save Himself and save man too.

"Except a corn [grain] of wheat fall into the ground and die,
it abideth alone."
JESUS COULD HAVE SAVED HIMSELF, BUT NOT MAN ALSO.

What if He had come down?*

*Gordon M. Hyde, "What if He Had Come Down?" The Youth's Instructor, 112 (March
24, 1964):12-16.

Some evidence of the drawing power of Christ on the cross was evident even as He hung there. Not that all responded favorably to that drawing power then or even at a later time. For many, however, the events of that infamous and yet infinite day were etched upon their memories and upon their souls, and ultimately they yielded to the heart tug of God's love in Christ Jesus. But even as He hung there, one who had little to lose in this life (for his was moving swiftly to its close) felt the magnetism of the God-man. Drawing, presumably, upon prior knowledge plus the little bits of evidence that reached him as he too hung in agony, he allowed the Spirit of Christ which "lighteth every man that cometh into the world" to piece things together for him. This companion in agony became perhaps Christ's greatest source of strength and comfort in the hour of His most desperate need as he requested Jesus to remember him when He would come in His kingly power. And from the Man so despised, so feared, so hated and also so loved, he received the assurance that very day, that very hour, as together they hung in apparent helplessness and hopelessness upon the cross, that he would indeed be with Christ in Paradise.

There were other hardened characters around the cross who felt the pull of Christ's godliness. One was none other than a Roman centurion trained in all the hardness and discipline of the Roman infantry. As he watched, fascinated, a scene which was undoubtedly not a rare one for him to witness, and saw and heard all that went on in connection with the crucifixion of this Galilean, he actually praised God and declared, "Certainly this man was innocent!" Luke 23:47, R.S.V. And if it was the same centurion who with his men kept watch over the tomb of Jesus when he saw the earthquake and what took place, he and his men declared, "Truly this was a son of God!" Matthew 27:54, R.S.V.

Two men in high religious positions had their lives permanently changed the day of the cross. We remember Nicodemus and his nighttime interview with the Lord early in Christ's ministry. He was the man to whom Christ explained the steps to salvation more fully, more clearly, more simply than to any other. The seed of God's love had seemingly lain dormant for three years in this man's heart; but now with the death of Christ Nicodemus comes boldly forth, using his influence and his wealth. Together with Joseph of Arimathaea he secured for the body of their newly espoused Lord a more than decent burial. (See John 19:38-42.)

The closest followers of Jesus were too distraught, too despondent, and too fearful to appear in strength at the cross. Apparently only the apostle John was there of the twelve. We recall that from Gethsemane they all forsook the Lord and ran away. Perhaps they came sneaking back to the cross, but only John is named, standing by the cross with the mother of Jesus and His mother's sister and Mary Magdalene. Their faith in Him though torn with grief and rent by terror was unwavering in love, and they were there. Can it be imagined that in the midst of His own soul-conflict Jesus made provision for His mother and in so doing expressed His confidence in the loyalty and dedication of His disciple, John? "Then he said to the disciple, 'Behold your mother!' And from that hour the disciple took her to his own home." John 19:26, 27, R.S.V.

The full meaning, and therefore the full tug of the cross, does not come home to anyone of us at first glimpse or as the result of a first glance. But a true and accurate picture of the cross will, under the stimulation of the Holy Spirit, draw all men to Him who gave Himself that we might have hope of life eternal.

Whatever the fears of Christ's apostles that kept them from boldly witnessing for Him at the site of the cross, they were neither forgotten by Him nor forsaken by Him. In the early morning of the third day the women returned to anoint the Lord's body. They found the tomb empty and the angel guards sent a gracious and merciful message to Peter, the one who during the night of the trials invoked his old foul language as a fisherman and tried to deny the fact that he was a follower of the Lord Jesus. A personal message was sent, "But go, tell his disciples and Peter that he is going before you to Galilee; there you will see him as he told you." Mark 16:7, R.S.V. And soon the disciples were worshiping their risen Lord. His very presence among them had demonstrated for them, contrary to their fears, that indeed He was a risen Saviour. They worshiped Him; and later, under the fullness of Pentecostal power, they declared Him fearlessly to the multitudes gathered in Jerusalem from every corner of the inhabited world.

It was Peter who became not only the spokesman for the apostolic band but the challenger of all the powers that had just crucified his Lord as he burned in upon the multitude the accusation that they, his hearers, had crucified the Lord of glory. So much so that "when they heard this they were cut to the heart, and said to Peter and the rest of the apostles, 'Brethren, what shall we do?'" Acts 2:37, R.S.V. That is what happens to men who do not resist the drawing of the cross of Christ. The fearful become courageous, the timid powerful, the poor of speech eloquent, the unbelieving confident. That is the heart tug of God's love, and it peaks for us at Calvary.

The message of Pentecost was that He who had been hung upon the cross between two criminals was indeed the Son of God, the promised Redeemer to come, the Messiah of the Old Testament prophets. He who had been slain on the cross was no longer dead but risen and ascended to heaven, from whence He shall come again to receive to Himself those who accept and do not resist the drawing of His love sacrifice. At that time He will purge from His universe once and for all the specter of sin and rebellion. He will make this world on which He had planted His cross a restoration of His original plan for it, a world-girdling Eden and the center of God's universal government. And the effect of the preaching of these certainties of the past and promises for the future under the impact of the promised Holy Spirit produced thousands of transformed lives. Day by day there was a rapid buildup of the church of Jesus Christ into which these new believers, who could draw on their past knowledge of the contemporary Christ, were baptized and accepted into the fellowship and doctrine of the apostles of Jesus Christ the Lord. Pentecost was a firstfruits vindication of the heart tug of God's love seen in the cross of Calvary.

4.The Gift of Repentance

If the drawing power of the cross of Jesus is not re- sisted, it will lead the believer in Christ's sacrifice to the foot of the cross in a deep sense of sorrow for his per- sonal part in nailing Christ to the cross. It will create in him or her also a sense of regret and grief for the sins of the whole human family which brought Christ to the reality of the cross.

Remembering that Christ's whole mission and mes- sage is for the restoration of man to the image of God in which he was created and to the relationship with God which he had at Creation, it will be quickly recognized that man's primary problem is the problem of sin. There- fore it is fully understandable that Christ's remedy for sin involves both sorrow for sin and a turning away from it. There cannot be anything casual about a believer's attitude toward sin, any more than there can be a casual attitude of a believer toward the cross.

It is impossible for anyone to have a shuddering view of the cross and at the same time take a flippant or casual view of sin. Sin is the one thing in all God's universe that a believer not only has the right to hate, but the necessity to hate. For God Himself hates sin. Not in the sense of blind, recriminatory hatred such as we humans most

66

generally exhibit but a hatred in the sense of a loathing for sin that caused Him to give Himself, even to jeopardize Himself and His position and power as God, in the plan to destroy that which He hated. (This divine jeopardy is beyond our capacity to define.) Again, God did not hate in the vindictive sense of getting even with the one (Lucifer) who initiated sin in the universe and brought all our grief, but He hated in the sense of having an uncompromising and incontrovertible attitude toward sin. Sin has to go. It has to be destroyed. It cannot survive in God's universe, because the presence of God is to sin a consuming fire. (See Hebrews 12:29.) God and sin cannot dwell together.

The first sinner, and those who sympathized with Him, were cast out of heaven in the beginning of the history of sin. This earth, which was then potentially peopled with those who were made in the image of God, became the new arena, the new focal point of the great controversy between Christ and Satan. And before we even breathe a suspicion that there was something unjust about allowing the controversy to become concentrated here, let us look back again at the cross. Let us also remember that there was no necessity for Adam or Eve to sin. Every provision had been made for them to continue to reflect the image of God perfectly; and, had they only given to the words and will of God a greater weight of significance than they gave to the deceptive words of the tempter, they could have moved forever beyond the reach of his temptations, as the redeemed ultimately will do in the kingdom where affliction shall not rise the second time. (See Nahum 1:9; see Revelation 12:7-9.)

Think of the relationship between the revelations of God's love for the sinner and the depth of the sinner's repentance for his sins and sinfulness. This relationship reminds me of my mother's most poignant demonstrations of her willingness to sacrifice herself that I might have more of what I thought I needed (and certainly desired). In those demonstrations I found my selfishness the most glaring and condemning. It was then that I found in my own heart and mind the deepest regret and sorrow for past wrongdoings, disobediences, and deceptions, no matter how small or large, that involved my mother. When it was the most obvious to me that she was sacrificing her own genuine needs to help me to meet my supposed needs, I found myself the most contrite regarding whatever in the past or the present had been grievous to her in my behavior. This perhaps illustrates in a very inadequate way the scriptural principle that the goodness of God leads us to repentance, as Paul puts it in writing to the Romans. (See Romans 2:4.)

Perhaps there is a chain reaction that tends to produce in so many Christians today a superficial experience in Christ—one that seems not to reach the depths of guilt, one that leaves so many chambers of the soul inaccessible to the cleansing power and blood of Jesus Christ. So many doors to certain chambers of the soul are marked "Private: No Admittance."

According to the apostle Peter, repentance is a gift of God and goes hand in hand with God's forgiveness of sin. And again it is reiterated that an awareness of what Christ has done in becoming our Peace, our Saviour, leads us to respond in repentance. "God exalted Him at His right hand as Leader and Savior, to give repentance to Israel and forgiveness of sins." Acts 5:31, R.S.V. It is not without significance surely that repentance and forgiveness are placed in such close relationship in this statement by the apostle Peter as he gave witness to the Jewish council of his necessity to preach the gospel no matter what the consequences to him or his brethren.

Some believers are much concerned as to the exact order in which repentance and forgiveness come in the Christian's experience. Might it not be possible that they come in successive waves but very closely related to one another? It is generally true, however, that God's forgiveness is His response to our repentance (or sorrow for and acknowledgment of sins), while our desire to acknowledge the sins and our capacity to be sorry are stirred by the manifestations of His kindness and love toward us. So there is no need ever to think of repentance as a rugged and exacting requirement that God uses to keep the sinner at a distance from Himself.

The invitation of Christ, "Come unto me, all ye that labour and are heavy laden, and I will give you rest" (Matthew 11:28), is open and unequivocal as a promise to all mankind. It expresses again the mission and message of Christ's residence here in our world in our human nature. Conversely it is not conceivable that forgiveness could come to a sinful heart that still cherishes its sin or fails to acknowledge sin. Forgiveness cannot come to one who has no real feeling of regret or grief over those things that wound the Son of God and put Him again to open shame. It cannot come to those who claim to follow Him but betray Him and deny Him by their words and actions, particularly by their cherishing of their old lives of sin, by keeping paths to old indulgences very clear and accessible.

John was one of those who wanted to keep a clear path open to old indulgences. We met him in our early ministry in a mid-western state. As he and his family attended a branch Sabbath School and began to receive Bible studies, he came face-to-face with the claims of Christ upon a repentant sinner. He heard the experiences of others who had come to recognize specific ways in which they had transgressed the will of God and who in their sorrow for these past transgressions (and in their desire to turn away permanently from them) had been willing to make restitution, to repay old debts, returning things borrowed and forgotten. John turned pale at the very thought.

As the Spirit of God brought conviction to his heart of the love of Christ, on the one hand, and of his own past life of sinful selfishness, on the other, John had a distinct conviction that there were many things that he needed to make right. He sought us out and asked, with such apprehension that his very life might have been at stake, how he could possibly make restitution for some of the things which he had done. He was a small farmer; but in his younger days, before his family came along, he had been something of a wild character in the community, riding around in a Western outfit, packing a pistol on his hip. He had seemingly feared neither God nor man. In the process of those early days he sometimes "borrowed" a piece of equipment from a neighbor and just wasn't too careful to return it when he was through with it. The truth was that he had some of that equipment lying around his place even at the time he was talking about it to us.

John's question was the same as that asked by some of Peter's hearers at Pentecost: "What must I do?" "How can I make these things right?" "If I go back and acknowledge to some of these people some of the things I have done, they could clap me in jail for it." He was deeply shaken both by the convicting power of the Spirit of God and by his fear of the possible consequences of his attempt to face the people he had wronged and to make things right.

As we prayed and studied with John, his faith laid hold anew of the promises of God in Christ Jesus. One day he cleaned himself up and took some pieces of equipment in the trunk of his car, some money in his wallet, some tracts in his pocket and began a tour of the old neighborhood, attempting to make amends for past transgressions. Wherever he went people graciously received him, and some were so impressed that the power of Jesus Christ had taken hold of John's heart and life that they demanded to be given some of the tracts in his pocket. One comparatively rough character grabbed the tracts out of his pocket and said, "If any of this stuff has done anything like this for you, John, maybe it will do me some good."

No one threatened to take John to court, and some would not hear of his making restitution for things which they had long forgotten. But all were glad to see this man's life transformed. His religion was proving to these neighbors (some of whom were not the best of Christians themselves) that true Christianity is a reality—a life-transforming reality that has real consequences in changing the life-style of the convert. They could see that John was not just caught up in some superficial, emotional experience. He was ready to put his pocketbook where his mouth was. He who had been almost a terror in the neighborhood was ready to acknowledge his wrongdoings of the past and even to risk serious consequences from the acknowledgment. Surely this was genuine repentance and perhaps its all-too-frequent absence from present-day revivals robs these so-called revivals of the power to transform other lives and to constitute a witness to the grace and mercy of God in Christ Jesus.

It isn't always the size or nature of the transgression

that is significant. On the one hand, with the apostle Paul, the fact that he had once persecuted the followers of Jesus Christ, putting them in jail, having them beaten and in other ways deprived of their rights and freedoms, left such an indelible impression upon his mind that a lifetime of consecrated service to Jesus Christ could never erase it. To the end of a life in which he repeatedly jeopardized his life for Christ, the apostle Paul just could not forget that he had once persecuted Christ in the person of His followers. In fact, it almost would seem that the longer he walked with Christ the more aware Paul became, the more sensitive he became, over his earlier life of rebellion against Christ. The more eagerly then he seized every opportunity to testify to what Christ had done for him in his conversion on the Damascus road and to the transformation which this had brought into his life. On the other hand, some of us who have been nurtured and sheltered from birth in a Christian home and family may have been protected by our very early environment from conspicuous and far-reaching acts of selfishness, yet even we, when our consciences have been made tender by the revelation of the love of God in offering the righteousness of His Son to be counted as our righteousness, have had our consciences made tender and our memories stirred as to past transgressions—large or small.

For example, in the British public transportation system as it was during my boyhood there were conductors on the buses to collect passenger fares and to issue tickets. Passengers proceeded to their seats and sometimes this would be "upstairs" on a double-decker bus. The conductor would repeatedly make his way through the bus calling for fares. Generally he had a fair idea who had just got on the bus and would come directly to that passenger for his fare. But sometimes, and particularly during a rainy day at rush hour, when the bus was overcrowded and a schoolboy was trying to get the last of his homework done on the bus, he might actually be overlooked by the conductor and even inadvertently find himself off the bus with his fare still in his pocket or in his hand. A small thing perhaps, just tuppence (something like a nickel). But these things came back to mind and memory and called for restitution. Little foxes spoil the vine. (See Song of Solomon 2:15.)

In those same high school days the Student Association sold "sweets" during play and lunch times, and the proceeds were used for various student projects. Upper-form students had the matter in hand, purchasing the sweets from a local sweetshop, handling the sales, and keeping the account. There was a device, however, by which an extra bar of Cadbury's chocolate might become available to the sellers, and that was if a bar were broken. Now, it did not require a particular ingenuity to find ways and means of "accidentally" dropping a box with the "unfortunate" cracking of a bar or two, whereupon these "unsalable" goods were consumed by the upper-formers who handled the project. Not much money involved. Perhaps a total of a few shillings over a period of two or three years, but a heightened conscience prompted by the love of God in Christ Jesus brought these things also back to memory and stirred a desire to make restitution. The desire was translated into action.

There may be some who would suggest that such carefulness is "straining at a gnat." The piece of fruit which Eve took from the forbidden tree in the Garden of Eden may not have been all that big, and it was "just once—just this once." But it brought "all this night and all our woe," and it brought Calvary's cruel cross. There is also the factor that as the conscience is made increasingly tender by the working of the Spirit of God upon the heart (in the manner in which Israel of old was commanded to "afflict their souls for sin" as they gathered about the sanctuary) the Holy Spirit has a way of peeling layer after layer of our memories back. Or to put it another way, He has the power to enable us to see as sin today what had not seemed so sinful, if sinful at all, yesterday.

This sensitivity reminds us of the sentiment of an M.V. leaflet that we had some years ago entitled, "Others May—You Cannot." (Perhaps it is available still.) And we referred to it many times in our children's growing-up days. They would want to know why certain people could do some things that we would not want our children to do. How could Elder So-and-So's children do this and get away with it, but Dad won't let us do it? And the only answer we had to that type of inquiry was that "others may—you cannot." And why not? (And this is where a delicate little problem of smug self-righteousness could creep in.) "Son," we would say, "God has called some things to some people's attention that He may not yet have called to other people's attention. But the responsibility of the party of the first part is created by what God has shown to him and brought to his attention." We used to try to assure the children that there were others who had higher standards than our own and who had consciences more tender yet than ours, for they had grown in grace farther or faster than we had. Nevertheless, we expected to grow more particular, more consistent, and more ardent in our devotion and consecration to the Lord, rather than less.

This was merely an outworking of the principle that the nearer we come to the Lord, the more clearly we see our own defects of character. And the more our consciences are instructed by the Word of God and the counsels of His Spirit to the remnant church, the more clearly we shall discern our errors and transgressions of the past and of the present. This very sensitivity to the overall process of penitence also acts in itself as a barrier against future transgression. The better informed the conscience, the less likely that the repentant sinner will blunder blindly into the old temptations and sins. The deeper the repentance—the more sensitive the conscience, the more fully it is instructed by the will and Word of God—the more likely that under the Spirit's guidance the right decisions and right choices will be made when confrontations with evil are pressed upon the believer in the days to come.

This is not to suggest that the Christian is earning merit or entering upon a legalistic relationship to the plan of salvation in the experience of repentance and restitution. He does not make amends in order to win the favor of God or merit eternal life. It is only as the love of the Godhead for the sinner comes home to his conscience and consciousness in the substitutionary life and death of Jesus Christ for him that true penitence leads to true restitution and restoration. Such repentance, induced by the love and mercy of God in making available the imputed righteousness of Jesus Christ, is a repentance that needs not to be repented of. It is Spirit-indited; it is genuine and it is true; and it is a response to the goodness of God.

This matter of repentance and restitution is a more troublesome one to the Christian when it involves repentance of an oft-repeated pet indulgence. It would be easy to say that these indulged weaknesses are inherited (without doubt in some instances the tendencies toward them could be inherited). But rather than looking for evidence in my ancestral tree of someone who has revealed the same weakness that has plagued my life, and being therefore inclined to excuse myself over his weakness, it could be safer and more wholesome and more a part of the spirit of true repentance for me to recognize that it has been *my* repeated indulgence of that tendency, if I inherited it, which has given it such strength in me.

We are all aware that a cord woven from two or three strands may be readily broken. Ten of the same strands might be almost impossible to break and twenty utterly impossible. So it is with our pet sins (and more than likely we each have one or more such). And in some instances there is no apparent rhyme or reason why that particular indulgence is our repeated downfall. And there is always the temptation to congratulate oneself that what bothers another and causes his downfall affords not even a slight temptation to oneself. But undoubtedly the enemy of God and man knows sufficient of both our heredity, our environment, and our past indulgences to bring the temptations of greatest potential to each one of us and particularly at times of greatest vulnerability—perhaps a time of discouragement or of Elijah-like despondency, of physical weakness and sickness, or a time of exhaustion from overexertion, even in the work of God. But as surely as we are each individuals, the tempter brings to us most frequently those sins which so easily and particularly beset us. And how do we relate to the Lord over these repeated indulgences of the one or more pet sins? How does true repentance operate in this situation?

We think of the question which Peter raised about how often one should forgive his brother, and how he thought he was being unduly righteous and gracious in suggesting that he might even bring himself to forgive his brother seven times, which was far beyond the rabbinical recommendation. But we remember Christ's answer that he should be prepared to forgive seventy times seven. Why would He say that? Presumably because 490 times would be often enough for the one wronged to forget the exact count of how many times he had forgiven. Certainly this can hardly be a call from the Lord for us to indulge our pet weaknesses 490 times, but may it not hold for us some ray of hope as to His long-suffering toward us?

But what would be a realistic and practical answer? Is it a matter of screwing up our courage tighter, applying our determination and will with greater force and conscious effort? Would it be found in making specific efforts to keep ourselves out of the realm of that particular temptation? Each of these and other factors might play a part in varying degrees in each individual case; but if it is the goodness of God that leads us to repentance of any sin, it surely must be the depths of His goodness alone that would lead us to genuine repentance for the most indulged sins. And if repentance includes the genuine sorrow for sin that leads us to bow at the foot of the cross in penitential acknowledgment of those sins, will that sorrowful confession not do more to intensify our loathing for that sin than any other factor? Would it not be a fuller and clearer revelation of the depths of God's love portrayed in Gethsemane and on Calvary that would have the greatest power to produce genuine sorrow for the most-cherished sins?

Without doubt we need to intensify our awareness of

the crucial nature of this issue which we are here discussing. We can do this by remembering that one need not transgress the whole law of God in order to be guilty of offending all, for he that offends in one point is guilty of all. This points us back to the principle at stake here. If the fulfilling of the commandments of God is based upon and is the fruit of the love of God—if love is the fulfilling of the law—then to proclaim my honor for the law and yet to indulge repeatedly in the breaking of one particular point is to say, "I love You, Father, but— I love You supremely and my neighbor as myself, but— I give You my whole heart and life and resources, but—" Would it not be logical, in such a case, that when God opens the gates of His kingdom to the redeemed and one of the "but" candidates approaches the gates of heaven, he would be told, "I would love to have you here in My kingdom, but—?" Surely when the individual clings to his treasured sin, he virtually says to God, "I love You supremely, but I love this little sin more. I believe that Jesus died on Calvary's cross to deliver me from the power of my sins, and I gladly yield them all to Him— except this one."

Perhaps, in many instances, we are not thinking such thoughts as these, not even formulating them in the mind, let alone expressing them with the tongue; but what *are we saying* by our actions and our attitudes?

What a comfort there is in the first and second chapters of John's first epistle, and how we need the reassurances! "If we say we have no sin, we deceive ourselves, and the truth is not in us. If we confess our sins, he is faithful and just, and will forgive our sins and cleanse us from all unrighteousness. If we say we have not sinned, we make him a liar, and his word is not in us. My little children, I am writing this to you so that you may not sin; but if anyone does sin, we have an advocate with the Father, Jesus Christ the righteous; and he is the expiation for our sins, and not for ours only but also for the sins of the whole world." 1 John 1:8 to 2:2, R.S.V.

We should go back and note that when our pistol-packing friend, John, of the Midwest, came to an awareness of what his past sins had been, he not only was sorry about them but he was ready to acknowledge his past wrongs at the risk of serious consequences and cost to him. And he added restitution to his acknowledgment. In other words, it was not a quick and flippant, "Oh, I am sorry," or "Excuse me." Rather, it was a heartfelt acknowledgment and confession. And whatever the indulgence—be it a pet one or an occasional one—the words of the wise man are alike true, "He who conceals his transgressions will not prosper, but he who confesses and forsakes them will obtain mercy." Proverbs 28:13, R.S.V. So repentance and confession reveal themselves as the counterpart to any cover-up. It is interesting to remember that from the commitment of the first human sin man has tended to hide himself in the depths of the garden away from God as though that could protect him from both God's omnipresence and omniscience (all knowledge everywhere).

We alluded to it very briefly earlier in this chapter, but Seventh-day Adventists have particular reason to be concerned with the parallelism between the experience of Israel of old and God's commandment-keeping people today in relationship to the biblical expression, "Afflicting the soul for sin."

To Christians who have lost all interest in the sacrificial system of the sanctuary and the temple of the Old Testament, this expression has likewise lost much if not all of its significance. And to the degree to which Seventh-day Adventists today may be forgetting the prominent place in their total faith of the teachings of the cleansing of the sanctuary, they too may be losing sensitivity to the significance of this expression related to experience of afflicting the soul for sin. Of what does it consist, and why is it so vital?

The typical system of the Old Testament gave a representation of the plan of salvation. Those who believed in the atonement that had been made and would be made were to come on the Day of Atonement particularly through the blood of the sacrifices offered. They were to surround the tabernacle (or later the temple) and search their hearts for sin. They were to search as diligently as would a woman in Old Testament times search her house with a candle, looking in the rush or dust floor for a lost article of value such as a ring or a jewel from her heirloom headpiece. There was to be an examination of the conscience, a calling out to God to turn the searchlight of His righteousness upon the soul. Even as an X-ray film of a diseased part of the body reveals the seat of the affliction or disease, the Holy Spirit reveals the infection of sin.

The people of Israel came yearly to the Day of Atonement experience in the typical service. The reality of the plan of salvation was only represented back there in the sacrificial system, but we today believe ourselves to be living in the time of the final work of Christ, our Advocate (as He is spoken of in 1 John 2:1). He is soon to conclude His work as our Advocate and to make the declaration: "Let the evildoer still do evil, and the filthy still be filthy, and the righteous still do right, and the holy still be holy. Behold, I am coming soon, bringing my recompense, to repay every one for what he has done. I am the Alpha and the Omega, the first and the last, the beginning and the end." Revelation 22:11-13, R.S.V.

It is not at all true that God is searching His books of record to see if He can find one unconfessed and unforsaken sin, which would justify Him in *excluding* us from His eternal kingdom and His eternal presence. Rather, He is searching for evidence of our repentance and our faith that would enable Him to impute to us the benefits obtained by the atonement rendered by Jesus Christ both in His death on Calvary's cross (on which He paid the price for our salvation) and in His ministry as High Priest since His ascension to heaven where He ministers at the right hand of God as our Advocate and Mediator until the final day of judgment is come.

There is an aspect of this work of repentance and confession with which many of us have a difficult struggle and for which we definitely need a solution. That problem lies in the reticence that we have and show toward confessing specific and real wrongdoings, and especially for confessing them to specific individuals who have suffered by our wrongdoings. In other words, we are very prone to want to use the blanket method with an acknowledgment to God or an acknowledgment to our fellowmen regarding our sins. It is much easier to write a general letter to a large group or body of persons than to a specific individual whom we have wronged. It is infinitely easier to say, "If I have hurt anybody in anything that I have said or done, I am sorry," than it is to go to a specific individual and say, "On such-and-such a day and under such-and-such circumstances, I did thus-and-so to you or said thus-and-so about you, and I am sorry for that and have come to acknowledge it, apologize for it, ask your forgiveness, and assure you of my intention to do everything possible to counter any false impression I created by what I did or said and to make amends in any other way that may be indicated."

Many of us would rather find some indirect way of making amends so that we show ourselves more concerned to make ourselves stop feeling bad about the case than really to clear it with the individual involved. It is quite generally thought that men find it virtually impossible to confess their wrongdoings to their wives, mothers, sweethearts, or children, and there is almost a traditional acceptance of a substitute confession or a substitution for confession. The individual who has done wrong will try to be "extra nice" in an attempt to atone for the past failures. The old saying that two wrongs don't make one right may need to be modified in order to have some application here.

If the individual feels the need to make amends for his past failures, good and well; but making amends can never substitute for the specific acknowledgment of the wrong involved. The one in error is actually short-changing himself by the substitute methods, because he will be blunting the keen edge of his conscience with a salving approach as opposed to making specific and direct acknowledgments which tend to sharpen and intensify the sensitivity of the conscience which in itself builds barriers against yielding to future temptations.

Let us hasten to add that there may be wrongs which should be acknowledged and confessed to God alone, where no other individual has been or could be specifically and directly harmed by the wrong. For example, the evil may have been in the realm of wrong thoughts or wrong motives, known only to the individual and his Lord. It may have been an instance of a lack of faith or of a spirit of murmuring and complaining against the Lord. It is important to limit the sphere of the influence of wrongdoing in every way possible while fulfilling also the biblical instruction to "confess your sins to one another, and pray for one another, that you may be healed." James 5:16, R.S.V.

There is another danger area that needs especially to be watched in our time when various "psychological" theories would encourage individuals to "hang out" their wrongdoing before others in group sessions or in various types of sensitivity sessions in which the individual is supposed to cast away all inhibitions and open his innermost self to the gaze of himself and those in his group. Unless those in his group have been directly affected and injured by whatever it is the wrongdoer wishes to confess, he not only has no obligation to acknowledge such to them but he may actually be doing them a disservice by so acknowledging, because it is easy for sinners to take even a salacious interest in the sins of others. And sometimes the sinner himself seems to derive a sort of reliving of the pleasure of his old sin by recounting it often (and there is a certain level of notoriety that can be derived by this recital of one's sins before others).

It is possible for a sinner to develop a type of moral exhibitionism, and surely only the evil one himself can be benefited by such an approach to repentance and confession. This is particularly true where the sins are of a moral nature involving matters of appetite and passion, or where the individual has lived heavily in and of the world and its lusts and pleasures. He certainly may wish to bear witness to others of the deliverance that the grace and power of Christ have brought to him, but in the process he does not need to whet the appetite of the innocent for his own past indulgences or run the risk of resurrecting his own old pleasure in sin by his repeated vivid recounting of it.

If repentance involves not only sorrow for sin but a turning away from it with loathing and a growing hatred of the sin that crucified the Lord of glory, then there cannot possibly be any strength or benefit in a reliving and a rehearsing of the old way.

If we wonder whether the apostle Paul with his persecution of the church would be an exception to this principle, we would only need to think of the difference between the nature of that type of sin and sins of a salacious or prurient interest.

But let us come back once more to the underlying principle of all in this matter of genuine repentance and confession and restitution. It is not an exercise in self-righteousness that makes these particular steps to Christ effective or even meaningful. It is the response of the sinful heart to the manifest love and mercy and forgiving grace of Jesus Christ that leads to genuine repentance—a repentance free from self-justification, free from offering excuses, free from self-centeredness of any variety and strong in a rejoicing in the mercy of God's grace through Jesus Christ our Lord.

5.A Life of Restfulness

Large families seem to thrive on lots of company and many friends. Ours was no exception. My boyood memories cover many a Sabbath day when our already above-average sized family was supplemented by visiting relatives, by individual friends of particular members of the family, by students from the nearby college, or by nurses from the nearby hospital as the case might be. And following a tasty and nourishing Sabbath lunch the group usually migrated to the living room or to the shaded lawn behind the house near old London, and a Sabbath afternoon discussion would frequently follow.

I must have been in my early teens when several minister members of our family and their wives and others were gathered in the living room around the cheery fireplace—that was an indispensable part of Sabbath day for us—and the topic turned to justification and sanctification. The ensuing discussion grew quite lively as individuals made attempts to explain or define the difference between these two aspects of the plan of salvation. As the youngest member of the family, I was prone to sit and listen if only for fear that if I became too much in evidence I might receive some suggestion about going elsewhere to read a book or going to take a walk or some other not-so-subtle method of removing me from the situation. So I learned to sit and listen and say very little at that stage of my youth. But eventually, prodded by one of my rare jabs of genius, I overcame my cultivated reticence. Finding a slight pause in the discussion, I pressed in my idea that sanctification seemed to me like justification in motion.

Over the years since then I have given much thought and some amount of study to this issue and have really not come up with a much better definition than I was able to offer at fourteen years of age. Or was it fifteen?

But certainly in the years of study and teaching and preaching since, I have been looking for and watching for a satisfactory clarification of this matter. As a result of teaching several sections of Life and Teachings of Jesus at the college level for a dozen years or more (and teaching academy Bible for a number of years before that), I have inclined to the view that the symbolic illustration of the vine and the branches, presented by Jesus to His disciples in the night of His betrayal, is as clear and complete and adequate an illustration of the relationship between justification and sanctification as I have yet found. For purposes of sharing this viewpoint with the reader, let us take a careful look at what Jesus was saying, as recorded in John 15:1-17.

The setting for this presentation would certainly seem to be the time when, following the last Passover service with His disciples in the upper room and following a considerable discourse with them there, Christ proceeded with His disciples toward the Garden of Gethsemane. In the available light of the full Passover moon the Lord could well have passed by a luxuriant vine with its leaves and fruit glistening, dew-laden, and bathed in the light of a brilliant moon. How typical and

natural it would have been for Jesus to point to the vine
clinging to its trellis—for a vine does not support itself
as does an oak or a cedar—and say to His disciples (a free
paraphrase):

"I am the true vine and My Father is the vinedresser or
gardener. If a branch does not bear fruit, the gardener
takes it away. If the branch does bear fruit, he prunes it
that it may bear more fruit.

"Now, you are branches of the vine and I am the vine.
You have been made clean or justified by the word
which I have spoken to you; and I want to urge you to
abide or rest in Me, and I will abide and dwell in you.

"You understand, even though several of you are
fishermen, that a branch cannot bear fruit by itself unless it remains attached to the vine which provides it
with life and nourishment. Let Me say again, I am the
vine and you are the branches. Now, if you live in Me
and I live in you, then you will bear a lot of fruit; but if
you try to live separated from Me, disconnected from
Me, severed from Me, you will not bear any fruit. In fact
if you don't live in Me (or any other of My branches that
will be grafted in later) you will not remain in Me, dwell
in Me, abide in Me. You or they will just dry up, dead,
and someone will come along and clean up the vineyard
and gather up the dead branches and throw them into
the fire and they will be burned.

"Now, if you will keep this living relationship with
Me and you will allow My Words to live in you, then
there is nothing that you need in order to do My work
and to be fruitful that I cannot do for you. This is what
will reflect the greatest glory to the Father, to the
heavenly Vinedresser, that you bear a great deal of fruit
and so demonstrate and prove and test the fact that you
are My followers.

"The relationship between Me and you is to be so close and so constant that I can say that as the Father has loved Me, that is the way I have loved you and I want you to keep it that way. Just abide, just rest, just trust in My love. For My love to you is the same kind as the Father has for Me.

"Now, I just said that by bearing fruit you will demonstrate that you are My disciples. Let Me go on to say, if you keep My commandments you will abide in My love. That again is the same as between Me and the Father, because I have kept His commandments and that is how I abide in His love and I want you to do the same with regard to Me.

"Even though I know what lies just ahead of Me and also each one of you, I have told you these things now so that you will have My deep joy living in you, so that you will be filled with joy.

"Now, if you are wondering about the nature of My commandments, let me share it with you once again. I want you to love one another in the same way that I have loved you. There is no greater love that a man can have than to lay down his very life for his friends. [And though Jesus had told them on several occasions that this is what He would do, they still were not prepared for it neither did they believe it. But that very night He would commence to do what He was now telling them about.] At this point I am not asking you to lay down your life for Me in order to prove that you are My friends, but I do ask you to do what I tell you as an evidence that you are My friends. Notice that I am calling you My friends and not My servants. You are more than servants, because I have shared with you everything that the Father has made known to Me. Please do not develop pride in yourselves when I tell you that you are branches

of Mine, that I am the vine and you are My branches—
because you didn't choose Me. You did not initiate this
plan that I am telling you about. Its success is not
guaranteed by you. It is guaranteed by Me and by the
Father. I chose you—at least eleven of you—and I ap-
pointed you that you should go and bear fruit as I have
been in the world to bear My Father's fruit, and I have
made plans so that your fruit will continue. There is no
need for it to fail, if only you will abide in Me.

"And because of the special close and intimate relationship between Me and you (and as long as you retain
that relationship by not at any time cutting yourself off
as though you could live without Me), you will be able
to ask the Father for everything that you need in doing
My work, living My life, bearing My fruit, and because
you will ask for it in My name—in the way that I would
ask for it were I in your place—He will give it to you.
Don't forget, love one another, because this is the heart
of My command to you."

There, in essence and with slight amplification, is
Christ's clearest and fullest presentation of the relationship between beginning a life in Him and continuing a
life in Him. And essentially that is the one difference
between justification and sanctification. Justification
takes place when the wild branch allows itself to be
severed from the old wild stock to which it belongs by
nature and, in response to manifestations of Christ's
love and the Father's love, chooses to become a part of
the vine, Jesus Christ. So by the sacrifice which Jesus
made of Himself (having lived a life of perfect obedience
to His Father's will), He offers a willing branch, a believing branch, the privilege to be disconnected from the
old setting and domination and to be grafted into the
true vine. And the Father or His agents, the angels, and

His Fellow Worker, the Holy Spirit, will undertake to secure the real, permanent life-connection between the vine and the branch. And yet the branch always retains the prerogative, the power to choose to leave the vine again. Were that not true, Christ doubtless would not have repeated so often His urging that the branches abide in Him.

At the same time the branch is not a perfectly and completely transformed branch at the moment that it is grafted into the vine—not even after the life of the vine begins to replace and take over the life functions of the branch fiber by fiber and vein by vein. Were that not true there would be no call for the Father to do any work of pruning. Were the branches perfect, fully developed without any of the old sinful tendencies left from the moment of being grafted in, there would be no pruning work necessary. But the heavenly Father who has allowed His Son to be separated from Him in becoming the Sin Bearer in our place—He undertakes to supervise the work of the pruning of the branches. Some of them grow too much wood and not enough fruit. Some grow too many leaves and so have not sufficient energy to produce fruit adequately. Some display sports of their old nature—wild and ungainly growth even after being grafted into the true vine and being counted and treated as part of the vine. Therefore, because of the relationship that exists by faith between the branch and the vine, the Father loves the branch in exactly the same way that He loves the vine (which represents His Son).

We have already talked in the previous chapters about faith, forgiveness, justification, the new birth, and conversion, and all of these phases of salvation are a part of the grafting-in process of the branches to the vine. Now the question is, What next? Where do we go from here? And for many of us there is the temptation (whether we put it into words or not) to feel that now we are established. Now we are Christians, we are converted, we are born again, we are regenerated. We have been forgiven for our past life of sin in response to our experience in repentance, confession, and restitution. Now we are justified. Now we may feel that (at least to some extent) we can do the work of the Lord on our own; we may think that we are not so dependent on Him for the life that we must live as His followers as we were in first coming to Him. There could be no more tragic error into which we could fall than such conclusions.

The Father and the Son and the Holy Spirit were all involved in our being grafted in. Why should we now think that we can live the Christ life on our own? Or perhaps, condescendingly on our part, with just a *little* help occasionally from the Holy Spirit.

It seems that the Lord had reason for so repeatedly insisting in these few verses of John's gospel that the branches *abide* in the vine. And there is a beautiful promise in prospect that when the branch chooses to abide and continues to make that choice daily and hourly, the Lord Himself reciprocates by His promises that He will abide in the branch and so there is a giving and a taking on the part of the branch. It gives itself over in utter dependence upon the vine. And it takes from the vine everything that it needs to be fruitful. And where the newly living branch begins to manifest some of its old inherent and practiced tendencies to evil the heavenly Gardener carries the knife. The trials, the difficulties, the sorrows, the disappointments of life are among the knives which the heavenly Father uses to prune the branches. Yet His one goal in pruning is to increase and improve the fruitfulness of the branch.

Now, the *ongoing* work, the daily living in Christ and His living in the branch, is virtually a continuation of the relationship established when the branch was first grafted in. It is an illustration of the ongoing work of sanctification which continues as long as the branch lives in the vine, and in this sense it is not too difficult to see in what way sanctification is justification in motion.

There can be no real or meaningful conflict between the processes of sanctification and justification, on the one hand, or obedience to the law of God on the other. It was through Christ's obedience to His Father's commandments and His willingness to be bruised and wounded for our transgressions that the provision was made whereby we could be grafted in through His wounds as scions of the true vine. This dwelling in Him, observing His commandments, doing His will would direct and motivate the life of each branch, causing it to bear fruit, more fruit, much fruit to the glory of the Father and the glory of the Son. And that is the process of sanctification. It follows upon the experience in being justified, and each is equally dependent upon what Christ has done in His keeping His Father's commandments. There never comes a time when the branch can say (and it certainly would not want to say) that its own fruitfulness is what now makes it part of the true vine. It was a part of the true vine from the first day that it was grafted in, and it is still part of the true vine in the day when the Lord transfers His fruitful vine to the heavenly kingdom. The branch was acceptable to the Father through the Son the first day, and it is acceptable to the Father through the Son on the last day. For there is no suggestion anywhere in this illustration, or in any other biblical explanation of sanctification, that there is a stopping place, that there is a point at which the branch can say to itself, "That is enough. Now I am perfect. I cannot become any more fruitful. My growth and fruitfulness have reached their zenith and I can now relax. Indeed I may now sever my connection with the true vine and go it alone." No such concept is anywhere suggested by the Lord Jesus Himself.

The whole relationship could be turned end for end to say that if the branch is not growing more fruitful each day and thus is not being sanctified, then such a condition is in itself evidence that the branch is not grafted into the true vine. Maybe it was once but it has failed to follow Christ's persistent instruction that the branch *abide* in the vine, that it remain in the vine, that it trust in the vine, that it shall depend upon the vine constantly and always, that it shall lean upon the vine. At some point it has felt itself too independent to need the continuing support of the life systems of the true vine and, whether it knows it or not, is in the process of drying up and withering. If it does not seek to be restored to its place in the true vine through the merits of the Saviour, then it will ultimately be destroyed by fire.

The branches do not heed the commandments of Jesus in order to purchase for themselves a niche in the true vine. It is because they have a niche in the true vine that they heed the Lord's instruction that they should do His commandments, that they should obey His will, that His word should abide in them to instruct them, to motivate them, to direct them, to bring the divine nature more and more fully into them through the exceeding great and precious promises which God has given us in Christ Jesus. (See 2 Peter 1:3, 4.)

We have entitled this chapter "A Life of Restfulness." This life of restfulness begins in the moment when the branch is grafted into the true vine and the true vine and the gardener undertake from that point onward the fruit-fulness and life of the branch. The acceptability of the branch to the gardener throughout its life is dependent upon the fact that it has chosen to abide in the vine. The *result* of this abiding is fruitfulness, and the fruitfulness is a demonstration and a manifestation of the fact that the branch is grafted into the vine and that the life of the vine has become the life of the branch. At no point is the fruitfulness of the branch the means of its abiding in the vine. It is an evidence that the branch is abiding in the vine. The means by which this whole process is begun and continues resides wholly and completely in the fact that the branch has heeded the instructions of Jesus that it abide in the vine.

Some may wish to ask, Which is more important—justification or sanctification? In one sense there is no contrast to be made, because they are each equally dependent upon a relationship between the believer and his Lord. One has primacy over the other in that justification has to precede sanctification. Conversion has to precede the life of holiness. The new birth is the means by which the new life of Christ begins to indwell the surrendered heart. As with the illustration given to Nicodemus, the new birth is something which comes from outside the believer. It comes from above and it comes as a response to his response to the sacrifice represented by the uplifted serpent in the wilderness, the sacrifice of Jesus Christ on Calvary's cross.

Some may wish to inquire whether, as the process of sanctification proceeds, there is need anymore for justification. In response we would say, if there is no way for the branch to determine when the work of sanctification is complete, at what point would the branch wish to say that its acceptability to the Father is now dependent upon itself? And if the vine connection was established by justification and the key decision of the branch is to *abide*, how can the fruit bearing become the ground of acceptability to God on the part of the branch?

In its most frequent biblical use, sanctification represents a setting apart, a being dedicated to holy use and purposes. (It can even be used negatively of that which is dedicated to an improper use and purpose.) So when the branch is grafted into the true vine, one might say that it is set apart to the purpose of fruitfulness—not its own fruitfulness—but the fruitfulness of the vine into which it is grafted.

It may seem to some that we are canvassing this subject too many times and from too many angles. It certainly is not with the purpose of confusing but rather of endeavoring to show that there is no point in the branch's experience when it can afford to claim acceptance with God on account of its own fruitfulness. That would be to take the focus of the branch's attention away from the true vine and to turn it inward upon itself. The secret of the branch's fruitfulness is in the abiding, in the receiving of the words of Christ, in the openness to the will and commandments of Christ, in its dependence upon Christ and its surrender to the pruning experiences permitted by the heavenly Father who handles the knife with skill and in love. The branch, after all, is a branch of His Son Jesus Christ, the true vine. Think not that the Father rejoices in the pain or suffering of the branch being pruned any more than He could rejoice in the sufferings of His Son as He dwelt here among men and finally paid the penalty for the sins of all men. Rather, the picture of the Father is that He could not endure the suffering of His Son; that all nature suffered and anguished with the Son in His sufferings;

that the Father hid Himself in darkness while reconciling man to Himself through the Son.

For purposes of our salvation, Jesus made Himself dependent on the Father as a vine is dependent upon some other means of support than its own self-support. He also submitted His will to the will of the Father. So there is almost a parallel here between Christ's attitude of dependence and submission in relation to His Father and what ours should be in relation to Christ. The most dangerous thing the branch can do is to harbor feelings of independence, of self-righteousness, of adequacy, of holiness, or of rebellion. It is under such circumstances that the branch would be the most inclined to sever its connection with the true vine unless it should deliberately and arbitrarily desire to return to the old life of sin which it knew before being grafted in. Then it might turn its back utterly and deliberately on the Lord.

There never was any suggestion of an illustration anywhere in the Old Testament sanctuary system that the prayers of the believer would be acceptable to God without the sweet incense of the righteousness of Jesus Christ, without the cleansing, sanctifying power of the blood that was shed. In fact, the constant lesson about the shedding of blood was that there is no remission or forgiveness of sins without the blood, and this requirement was not given a time limitation or a conditioned limitation with respect to the believer. Neither Moses, nor Aaron, nor any of Aaron's descendants could appear in the house of God without the intervening incense, the intervening cloud of incense. It is true that Moses himself, on the mountaintop, came the closest of any man to receiving a personal revelation of the person of God; but this was shared with no one but himself, and he was shielded from the fullness of divine glory.

In the sanctuary system the blood and the incense were always needful, always a requirement of approaching to God. And if it is true that the closer a believer comes to Christ the more faulty he appears in his own eyes, then he will be more and more inclined to say with Paul, "I am chief of sinners," and he will become convicted of that more rather than less. And so he will look back with ever-deepening gratitude to the day when in Christ Jesus he was accepted by God as though he had never sinned. He will desire an unbroken relationship with God through faith in the Son. He will desire a constant update of this relationship. He will want to make this his first work every morning and his last work every evening and a continued work during every day.

If it be asked whether both the beginning experience of justification and the continuing experience of sanctification may be seen as a part or parts of the experience of righteousness by faith, it should be answered that the only righteousness man can ever bring to God originates in Jesus Christ and is shared with the believer whether through justification or sanctification in response to the believer's faith and trust in and dedication to Jesus Christ. A James may come along and demand that the believer demonstrate the fruitfulness of his faith by his works. In the judgment the judge may separate the sheep from the goats on the basis of what they have done or not done for him in the persons of their fellowmen, but these works and these obediences are never presented as the ground of acceptance with God but as the fruit and proof of the ground of faith found in the justifying righteousness of Jesus Christ and counted to us for righteousness. The fruit is produced in us by the indwelling of His Spirit.

And if it be felt that the words of James in his epistle

are unessential and contradictory to the gospel, one need only consider their application to the kinds of revival that are seen throughout the Christian world today (especially under the charismatic influences) where the cry is, "Only believe! Only believe!" Apply the words of James to the claim that is made of being acceptable to God through Jesus Christ without any regard for or consideration of the fruit of that belief in the life of the believer. (See James 2:14-26.)

For a life of restfulness, come and be grafted into the true vine. "Looking unto Jesus the author and the finisher of our faith." Hebrews 12:2.

6.Likeness to Christ

We have just spent an entire chapter in contemplation of the divine plan for creating fruitful disciples of the Lord Jesus Christ and have studied particularly the living illustration of the vine and the branches. We have seen the requirement that the branches abide in the vine and the consequence of that requirement in fruitfulness, in bearing fruit. We might well ask, What kind of fruit is borne by the branches of the true vine? It would seem self-evident that the fruit would be the fruit which Christ bore in His life, only now it is being borne in the lives of His disciples. And thus it proved to be, historically, when the apostles of the Lord began to bear witness to the multitudes, first in Jerusalem, then in Judea, then in Samaria, and then reaching out to the uttermost parts of the earth. They began to teach the people what Jesus had taught plus the messages of the resurrection and ascension—aspects which Christ could not preach effectively because these events had not yet taken place. They began to do the same works that He had done, and very quickly people took note of them that they had been with Jesus and had learned of Him. (See Acts 4:13.)

In the same cluster of discourses in which the parable of the vine and the branches is located, we have the three or four passages in the gospel of John that portray for us the promised work of the Holy Spirit. In these passages the Holy Spirit is called *parakletos* (see John 14:16, 26; 15:26; 16:7), which in some versions is translated "counselor," or in the K.J.V., "comforter." The verb from which the noun is derived carried such meanings as to encourage, exhort and comfort, and the noun *parakletos* has come to signify someone who intercedes for another, someone who helps. We have already referred to 1 John 2:1 where the same word appears and is used of Christ and is translated "advocate."

In these passages from John's gospel concerning the Holy Spirit, Jesus promises that the Comforter will do for His disciples what He Himself has done while He has been with them. Jesus reminds them that He is to leave them and return to His Father; but He assures them that He will not leave them orphans but will come to them in the person of the Holy Spirit. Not only will He, Christ, come to them, but the Holy Spirit will also bring the presence of the Father to abide in them. For Jesus, the promise of the Comforter was the greatest bequest that He could leave to these humble men in whose hands would reside the human aspect of the destiny of the gospel of the kingdom when Christ Himself should no longer be on earth to proclaim it. And He even indicated that it would be in the best interest of the disciples, and of the church, that He Himself should go away and send them the Comforter. Most obviously it was to their advantage because the Comforter would not be restricted by the limitations of humanity in time and place as was Jesus through His incarnation. By the ministry of the Holy Spirit, Jesus and the Father could be with every disciple anywhere and at all times throughout the world and even until the end of the world.

The coming of the Comforter was to be intimately associated with the fulfillment of the gospel commission because, as the Spirit of truth, the Spirit would continue to guide the disciples into all truth and particularly enable them to understand things which their unbelief had hindered their understanding directly from Jesus. Also, the fuller implications of the work which Christ had done in His life, in His death, and in His resurrection, would be brought to their understanding by the ministry of the Spirit of truth. In everything the Spirit would teach them and would enable them to do, glory would be brought to the Son and to the Father.

And so, having been led, and in the process of being led into all truth, the disciples would become witnesses, fearless and effective witnesses of Jesus, for they had been with Him from the beginning of His ministry and they would be able to tell from experience what He had said and what He had done. The Holy Spirit would remind them of those things which they might have forgotten and clarify their understanding of those things which had seemed dark and mysterious to them because of their unbelief and limitations.

So we may wonder, as we did at the beginning of this chapter, what was the nature of the fruit that would be borne in the lives of the disciples as branches of the true vine? Surely it would seem, from the closely associated promises of the Holy Spirit which Christ gave His disciples in His final discourses, that the fruit borne in their lives would undoubtedly be "the fruit of the Spirit." And it is through the apostle Paul that we have the most complete presentation of the cluster of fruit in the believer's life which is designated as the fruit of the Spirit. Perhaps some have placed too much significance on the fact that the term "fruit" is used in the singular form here in Galatians 5:22, 23. Students of the Word have seen the clustering concept in this wording. They have also thought of the fruit of the Spirit as being likened to a precious stone having many facets which together constitute one complete and precious stone but with many different reflecting faces.

Be that as it may, the lives of the apostles and of those who should come to believe on Christ through their word were to be marked by the fruit of the Spirit—"love, joy, peace, patience, kindness, goodness, faithfulness, gentleness, self-control." The inspired evaluation is that "against such there is no law." Galatians 5:22, 23, R.S.V. And that is as we would expect it to be—the fruit borne by the branches of the true vine would be fruit that would harmonize with the law of God (the expression of His character in human affairs and ways). And we could well ask how there could be any law that could condemn the fruit of the Spirit when the first item in the cluster is love. We remember immediately that love is the fulfilling of the law. Romans 13:10.

In his letter to the Galatians the apostle is contrasting the fruit of the Spirit with the works of the flesh. These works are not a clustering as the fruit of the Spirit, for any one of them is sufficient for a sinner's condemnation. (See Galatians 5:18-21.) These works of the flesh will ban those who indulge in them from an inheritance in the kingdom of God, and they are not a pretty listing—"immorality, impurity, licentiousness, idolatry, sorcery, enmity, strife, jealousy, anger, selfishness, dissension, party strife, envy, drunkenness, carousing, and the like." And the fruit of the Spirit is presented in contrast: "And those who belong to Christ Jesus have crucified the flesh with its passions and desires." Verse 24.

So again, far from the Lord's expecting and demanding of His disciples that they bear fruit by their own efforts or produce their own works of righteousness, He has made provision through the indwelling Spirit for the lives of His disciples to be filled with the fruit of the Spirit, and that is the same as having the fruitage of Jesus Christ Himself in the heart and in the life.

In the same manner that James taught that the law is a unity, and showed that the violation of any part of it is a manifestation of disharmony with the character of God's love (see James 2:10), so with respect to the fruit of the Spirit there is no part of the total cluster that is dispensable, no matter what the time or the circumstance in which the disciple of the Lord is called to live. In fact, the more contact the individual has with others the greater his need for the fruit of the Spirit in his life. For the characteristics of this fruit are largely the characteristics of sound and gracious interpersonal relationships and of reactions between the believer and those brought into contact with him.

Have you seen individuals whose lives have just been surrendered to the Lord Jesus Christ, individuals who have just laid hold of eternal life by faith in Christ's righteousness and by submission to His will? Have you seen such lives swiftly transformed by the fruit of the Spirit? Not that the fruit is fully developed or perhaps even balanced in its development at the outset, but as the life is opened increasingly to the Spirit and to the truth of Jesus as enunciated in the Word and in the counsels of the Spirit, these various aspects of the fruit of the Spirit come to be seen with increasing clarity, power, and forcefulness in the life of the trusting and committed follower of the Lord Jesus Christ.

Important principles of truth appear in the context in

which the fruit of the Spirit is listed by the apostle Paul in his writing to the Galatians, and it will be profitable to spend a little time in contemplation of this context and of the important principles relating to the law and to the gospel, the law and the Spirit, which are here enunciated.

Paul is writing to Gentile Christians and is encouraging them to retain the freedom or liberty with which Christ had made them free by His life, His death, and His resurrection, and His ministry as our Mediator at the throne of God. Some among the Christians who had a Jewish background were trying to encourage, if not compel, the Gentile believers to adopt certain of the requirements of the Old Testament in the ceremonial system, such as the practice of ceremonial circumcision, the sign which God had given to Abraham to distinguish his descendants from those of the nations round about them. The apostle pointed out to these Gentile believers that if they thought that after being justified (counted righteous) through the righteousness of Jesus Christ they could now justify themselves more by obedience to the circumcision law, for example, they would be making a bad bargain, for they would virtually be placing themselves under obligation to fulfill the whole law. (See Galatians 5:1-3.) He insisted that those who would be wanting to justify themselves by law would be severed from Christ. This expression reminds us of John 15 where fruitful branches that wish to make themselves independent of Christ wither and die and ultimately are burned. Those who would try to justify themselves through obedience, through legal requirements—and in principle this would apply to any law and any requirement of God for His children—would thereby be falling away from grace. (See verse

4.) Such a tragic condition should prompt sober reflection on the part of any Christian.

It is through the Holy Spirit, the apostle explained, that by faith we wait for the hope of righteousness. It is the Holy Spirit that awakens the new life in the believer. As Jesus explained to Nicodemus, we must be born again, born from above, born of the Spirit, and by faith in the righteousness of Jesus Christ wait for the fulfillment of righteousness in our lives in Him. Because, says the apostle, in Christ Jesus it is not whether we are circumcised or not circumcised that is of any account now in the times of the gospel, but it is "faith working through love." Verse 6, R.S.V.

That the apostle is thinking of more than the law of circumcision which came within the ceremonial symbolic system of the Old Testament becomes evident as he develops his argument further. He reminds the Galatian Gentile believers that in Christ they were called to freedom, but he begs them not to use that freedom as an opportunity to indulge the flesh. By that he would undoubtedly refer to the works of the flesh, especially human tendencies included in the seeking righteousness through one's own efforts. Rather than using your freedom as an opportunity for the flesh, says the apostle, "through love be servants of one another. For the whole law is fulfilled in one word, 'You shall love your neighbor as yourself.' " Verses 13, 14.

Here we recognize that the apostle is enunciating the same principles which Christ discussed with the lawyer (as we commented on that situation in an earlier chapter). The Ten Commandments we have seen summarized in the two principles of loving God supremely and one's neighbor as oneself, and it is to this latter basic principle governing relationships within the human family that the apostle is especially referring. Here he has definitely moved away from a mere ceremonial consideration and is dealing with the moral principles of the eternal law of God—the law of love, the law which is an expression of God's very character.

Paul now develops his line of reasoning farther, distinguishing the life of the believer in the Spirit and the life of the believer in the works of the flesh. He portrays a perpetual warfare between the desires of the flesh, on the one hand, and the desires of the Spirit, on the other, "For these are opposed to each other, to prevent you from doing what you would." Verse 17. We need to remember that the works of the flesh may not only involve the fleshly lusts of passion and intemperate appetite; but the works of the flesh can also involve religious activities in which self seeks righteousness through its own efforts rather than through faith in the imputed righteousness of Jesus Christ which brings the indwelling of the Holy Spirit into the believer's heart and life.

Paul then makes a statement which could easily be misunderstood and misinterpreted: "But if you are led by the Spirit you are not under the law." Verse 18. This verse and similar statements of the apostle's have been misunderstood and misinterpreted in a most unfortunate way over the centuries by those who would see in the gospel of Jesus Christ, and in His justifying righteousness, a deliverance from all accountability to and responsibility to the law of God as enunciated in the Ten Commandments and most clearly exemplified in the life of Christ. And here there is a delicate line that can easily be bent out of shape or moved out of place between the fruit of the Spirit on the one hand and legalism on the other, where legalism is defined as the effort to be righteous through one's own works of righteousness in attempted obedience to requirements of God. To know what the apostle had in mind in saying that if one is led of the Spirit he is not under the law, it is essential to read on into the words immediately following where he lists the works of the flesh on the one hand and clusters the fruit of the Spirit on the other. Having listed the works of the flesh, he warns, "Those who do such things shall not inherit the kingdom of God." Verse 21. Whereas when he has listed the fruit of the Spirit, he declares, "Against such there is no law. And those who belong to Jesus Christ have crucified the flesh with its passions and desires." Verses 23, 24.

He therefore who is led of the Spirit is not under the law in the sense of not being under its condemnation, because the works of the flesh are no longer the identifying marks of his life and character. He has turned his back upon the works of the flesh and has placed his complete trust in the perfect works of Jesus Christ lived out here on this earth. (Christ was He who could ask His enemies, "Which of you convicts me of sin?" John 8:46, R.S.V. And none of them could answer.) He who places his confidence in this righteousness of Jesus Christ is simultaneously justified, born again, regenerated, forgiven of his past life of sin, adopted into the family of Christ, grafted into the true vine, and brought under the leading of the Spirit.

Such a person is no longer under the law as condemned by it, because he has chosen to be under another law, the law of the Spirit. When the Law of that Spirit, and the leading of that Spirit, and the indwelling of that Spirit, take effect in the human heart, then the beautiful fruit of the Spirit is seen. When we look at the cluster of the fruit of the Spirit, we can see why there is no law that could possibly condemn him whose life is marked by such fruit. Let us ask: Would you not like to be working for someone in whose life the fruit of the Spirit is seen? Would you not like to be married to someone in whom the fruit of the Spirit is seen? Would you not like to be the son or the daughter of someone in whose life the fruit of the Spirit is seen? Would you not like to have a pastor or a church elder or a Bible teacher in whose life the fruit of the Spirit is seen? In other words, in any human relationship would you not like to be associated with those whose lives are marked by the fruit of the Spirit? It scarcely needs to be mentioned that you could likewise believe that others would be very grateful should they be forced to associate with you and then find the fruit of the Spirit in you. Look at this cluster of fruit once again—"love, joy, peace, patience, kindness, goodness, faithfulness, gentleness, self-control." What law could condemn a life so marked?

We should turn this equation around to show that a life in harmony with the laws of God is not a harsh, arbitrary, unlovely, awkward, sanctimonious, pharisaical, Victorian life. It is a life marked with all the beauty and loveliness of the character of Jesus; but it is not a soft, flabby life either. It is not a life bereft of principle; for it is a life of goodness, faithfulness, and self-control (also listed in the K.J.V. as temperance). If we would know what a Spirit-led life would really be like, then we have to study more and more of the life of Jesus, for there we have a life fully and completely led of the Spirit in every particular and under every circumstance.

Would we know how severe the battle with the flesh might be for those who would be led of the Spirit (for they are not taken out of the flesh physically when they are born again)? The apostle indicates that those who belong to Jesus Christ have *crucified* the flesh with its passions and desires. Verse 24. And this reminds us of all that Jesus experienced in going to Calvary and the cup that He drained in Gethsemane when He became our Sin Bearer, moving on to bear our sins to the tree. There is no place in the Spirit-led life for self-indulgence, whether of appetite, of passion, of temper, or of domineering characteristics. These characteristics belong to the flesh and the devil, not that the flesh of Adam was innately wicked, but it is fallen through sin. The appetites and drives, under the control of the Spirit, are not evil, for our Lord hungered and thirsted and was weary as we are. Before sin ever entered the world, He bestowed the gifts of appetite and of marriage upon the human family. There is no room here for the medieval concept of the innate wickedness of the body and of a separate entity, as the soul, alone being acceptable to God.

What we are trying to say here is that the Christian who walks the closest with the Lord will be the most Christlike individual that we have ever known or met. For love is the fulfilling of the law, and "the whole law is fulfilled in one word, 'You shall love your neighbor as yourself.' " Galatians 5:14, R.S.V.

This is truly a far cry from the strange stereotyped concept that many of us carry regarding a Spirit-filled life. We may think of it as a monastic life, as a life of joylessness, a life of negativism, a life of restriction and constriction. But rather the Spirit-led life is a life that reflects with increasing clarity and increasing detail the image of the Lord Jesus Christ Himself. It is a balanced, wholesome, outgoing, vibrant, and virile life. It appreciates beauty and creativeness in art, music, nature, literature, and every productive and positive human endeavor. And when we speak of such things, we may find ourselves wondering about the *gifts* of the Spirit, especially in this so-called charismatic age in which we are now living. We shall reserve our thoughts about these for the following chapter.

7. The Gifts of the Spirit

Without any doubt, the so-called charismatic movement of our time is a most remarkable religious phenomenon. It has brought about a type of unity among churches which years of effort by the World Council of Churches and the National Councils of Churches have not been able to achieve.

The charismatic movement derives its name from its claim to have within it the gifts (charismata) of the Holy Spirit. And this concept is derived from the New Testament, particularly from First Corinthians 12 through 14, Ephesians 4, and Romans 12. We frequently speak of these charismata as spiritual gifts. Whereas they are discussed the most fully and listed the most completely in the references just given, it is interesting to note that some of these particular gifts were in a measure bestowed on the apostles of Jesus during their missionary journeys—both of the twelve and of the seventy—and were promised by the Lord as aids to the accomplishment of the gospel commission which He entrusted to His apostles. This is most fully presented in the closing portion of Mark's gospel, chapter 16, verses 15 to 20.

In mentioning this Scripture we acknowledge that not all the ancient manuscripts include these particular verses of Mark's gospel, but textual witnesses attest to these verses, and there is increasing scholarly support today for their authenticity and inclusion within the canon of the New Testament. Certainly what was promised here by Jesus to His apostles found its fulfillment both at Pentecost and subsequently as recorded in the Acts of the Apostles and as mentioned by the apostles in their epistles to the churches.

It may be most significant that in the promising of particular gifts to those who would carry His gospel message, Jesus said, "These signs will accompany those who believe." Mark 16:17, R.S.V. And He directly linked the manifestations of these signs or wonders or miracles with the preaching of the gospel in all the world. He reiterated that those who would believe the message as presented and would be baptized would be saved, and that those who declined to believe would be condemned. The emphasis here is upon faith and acceptance of the gospel promises. The stress is not upon works of righteousness to be rewarded with miracles—no encouragement here for the thought that miracles could be performed by ecclesiastical saints. These signs and wonders were not designed merely to draw attention to those with whose work they would be associated. These signs were intensely practical, particularly with the situation confronting the infant church where largely uneducated men who would be without the advantage of a study of languages, for example, were to carry a message, a story, to give eyewitness testimony regarding the unique and remarkable life, the life of Jesus Christ, to "the whole creation." Verse 15.

Who would translate for these humble believers on the Lord Jesus Christ? And if they had no translators, how would they get the message out into new territory?

They had no printing presses, no means for the rapid dissemination of a message, no mass media of any kind. Everything would be conveyed by word of mouth except as groups developed, and then letters might be sent to be read in the groups. But who would provide the front edge of the gospel communication to new peoples with new languages—new to the apostles and their converts? The Lord anticipated this need and made provision to meet it in His promise.

The lives of the apostles would be in jeopardy from the kind of dangers which threatened lives in those days—poisoning, poisonous snakes, sickness and disease in a time when there was virtually no medical practice worthy of the name. How would these humble people be preserved and protected, traveling out to the world with the gospel of Jesus Christ?

We see all of these things exemplified in varying degrees in the Acts of the Apostles and in the epistles where there are references to narrative events. Pentecost was the initiation, perhaps, of these gifts, particularly the gift of languages. Again the gift met a very practical need in that here was a unique opportunity for the apostles to give the gospel message to thousands of people gathered from many different lands and who spoke and used many different languages. Through the gifts of the Spirit, as recorded in Acts 2, the apostles were endowed with the ability to communicate in these many different languages at a time when interest in the Galilean who had been crucified and who reportedly had been raised from the dead was at its height and was of concern to the multitude who had come up from Jerusalem for the annual feasts. It was an evangelistic opportunity par excellence, and the Spirit of the Lord made provision for the apostles to capitalize on it.

As the gospel message moved out through Judea and then into Samaria and then into the uttermost parts of the world, we can see with the widening circle how the particular gift of languages (or of tongues, as it is called) moved out with them. Likewise miracles of healing were an early part of the apostolic ministry. Signs and wonders truly did follow those that believed, and they not only provided practical means to meet practical needs but they served as an endorsement of the gospel message and of the faith of the apostles and disciples.

Something of a shadow is cast over these gifts of the Spirit by church historians who wonder why these gifts disappeared from view for so many centuries. But we would have to remember that the gospel itself largely disappeared from view during those same centuries. Heresies and schisms came in to afflict the church. A great apostasy transpired within a very few centuries, and the true church of Jesus Christ went into the wilderness phase portrayed by John the Revelator in Revelation 12 and particularly verse 6. It may also be assumed that in some measure the need for some of these gifts may have eased as the gospel reached out into many lands and converts came in who had a knowledge of the different languages in which the gospel had to be preached and published.

Naturally the question is raised as to why whole centuries passed without any significant and reliable record of the continuation of these gifts in the church. Again we must remind ourselves that many centuries went by under the domination of an apostate church, and not until the coming of Martin Luther and his immediate predecessors and successors was there a revival of the preaching of the true gospel of salvation through faith in the righteousness of Jesus Christ. With that revival of the true gospel there was undoubtedly some revival of spiritual gifts, although records of such are meager and perhaps the need for such gifts was overshadowed by the precious reclaiming of the gospel itself.

As we come down to our own day, the question may be asked as to the degree to which these spiritual gifts are evident in the church today. And here, in the history of the Seventh-day Adventist Church, we have a most interesting situation. For one thing from the very inception of this particular branch of the church of Jesus Christ there was manifest in the midst of it one of the gifts of the Spirit, the gift of prophecy, which has been a guiding influence, a building influence, a stabilizing influence, a unifying influence as this church has moved out into every corner of the earth in the final proclamation of the everlasting gospel.

Another major facet of the work and experience of this church has been the development of a program of healthful living in recognition of the fact that the body is the temple of the Holy Spirit and that it must be preserved in the best possible health as a fit dwelling place for the Spirit and as a fit instrument to represent the wholeness of the gospel message with its power to restore the whole man physically, mentally, spiritually. Thus in conjunction with the work of prophecy there were early calls through that gift of prophecy for the development by the Seventh-day Adventist Church of a work of physical healing and restoration and for the prevention of disease. In a measure this work has found its fulfillment in the chain of hospitals, sanitariums, clinics, health food factories, and restaurants scattered around the world. But let us go back and look at the promised gifts of the Spirit in the New Testament in order to understand their significance a little more fully and the relationship between the gifts of the Spirit and the fruit of the Spirit.

In First Corinthians 12 through 14 we have the most complete consideration of spiritual gifts to be found anywhere in the Scriptures, and we dearly wish that we knew to what questions specifically the apostle Paul was responding in writing his two letters to the Corinthian church. But we are left to a large degree to conjecture as to what these questions were. We know of a surety that the Corinthian church had received the gospel message in power and in fullness. It had been adequate to bring them out of the paganism and heathenism that beset their city and its environs. But in some way it is obvious that spiritual gifts were either being abused in the Corinthian church by misuse or that there were some counterfeits or distortions of true spiritual gifts. It is difficult to be certain just what the situation was, and it may remain impossible to ascertain it with certainty. Nevertheless, in these three chapters we find an enunciation of some vital principles which are applicable today regardless of whether or not we have perfect agreement as to the exact nature of some of these gifts and particularly the gift of tongues as seen in the Corinthian church.

The most logical explanation of tongues in Corinth happens to match the principle of the unity of the Scriptures, and it should be noted that there is no distinction whatever between the term used by the apostle Paul in writing to the Corinthians and in the term used by Luke in describing the tongues experience at Pentecost. Yet there were terms which the apostle Paul could have used in the Greek language to describe distortions of a true gift of languages, had that been the situation and had he wished to use such terms. He did not use them.

But what we are primarily looking at here is the fact that in chapter twelve the apostle lists the gifts of the Spirit and particularly stresses that their operation in the church was designed to unify the church, to build up the church, and that there should be no strife or jealousy because one member had a different gift from another. Paul used the illustration of the human body with its many different parts, with their varying functions, each equally essential to the whole, though different. In the thirteenth chapter he makes a most important declaration and enunciation of a vital and basic principle—that whatever one's actual spiritual gift and whatever his claimed spiritual gift, if his life were not governed by and motivated by love—the true love of God in Christ Jesus—then his gift would be nothing or worse than nothing. Here we see a remarkable link between the gifts of the Spirit and the fruit of the Spirit, in that love happens to occupy the first place in the listing of the cluster of the fruit of the Spirit in Galatians 5:22, 23.

It is after he had shown the supremacy of love over any and all of the gifts of the Spirit that the apostle moves into what is the fourteenth chapter to discuss in detail issues and problems connected with the exercise of the gift of tongues in the Corinthian church. There are those who see this gift as the Pentecostal gift of tongues being misused or misapplied in the worship situation and group situation of the Corinthian believers. Others feel that this was a diversion from, if not a perversion of, the Pentecostal gift that was being manifested among the Corinthians—a modified, if not false gift of tongues, that was bereft of meaning. They believe that Paul was not dealing with real languages but was denouncing a type of emotional experience, if not an excess, that revealed itself in some type of ecstatic sound that may or may not have been meaningful even to the one exercised by it and certainly may not have been understood by those within hearing. In either case the principles or rules which the apostle laid down in this fourteenth chapter to govern the exercise of this gift in a worship situation would certainly give no place to the ecstatic type of tongues experience which is being advocated in the charismatic circles today.

The apostle seems to suggest some kind of scale of value in the gifts of the Spirit in his listing of them—particularly in verses 27 to 31 of First Corinthians 12. Here he gives a numerical value—first to the apostles, second prophets, third teachers, then a listing of other gifts, the last of which is "speakers in various kinds of tongues." Verse 28, R.S.V. And he exhorts them: "Earnestly desire the higher gifts." Verse 31. Whether by the higher gifts he is contrasting, for example, the gift of apostleship against the gift of tongues, the last in the list, or whether he might be anticipating the thirteenth chapter in which he is showing a more excellent way than even the higher gifts—and that would be the way of love—we perhaps cannot be certain. The manner in which he introduces the gift of love would tend to suggest that within the list of the gifts of the Spirit (with which he has been dealing) there is an order of higher and lower. And if there be any significance to this ordering by the apostle, then the supremacy given today to the gift of tongues (genuine or not) is out of harmony with the New Testament emphasis. The top emphasis should be on apostleship.

Another aspect of this question that is of vital concern to Seventh-day Adventists today is whether these gifts are now seen in the remnant church, whether they will

be seen, and whether they ought to be seen. One principle needs to be enunciated at the outset: The reception
of any gift of the Spirit is not a measure of one's relationship to Jesus Christ through the gospel. The gifts of the
Spirit are the Spirit's gifts; they are under His control.
They are bestowed by the Spirit. This the apostle reiter-
ates throughout the twelfth chapter. And the Spirit dis-
tributes these gifts to each believer on the basis of the
Spirit's determination and selection. It is not for the
church or for any member of the church to judge another
because he does not have a particular gift. "All these are
inspired by one and the same Spirit, who apportions to
each one individually as he will." Verse 11, R.S.V.

It is vital to recognize and reiterate this great principle
today, because so many wish to equate the bestowal of a
particular gift, namely the gift of tongues, with being
baptized of the Holy Spirit or being filled with the Spirit
or being led of the Spirit. And for this claim there is no
adequate biblical support. Should each believer reveal
the *fruit* of the Spirit? Yes! When the apostle lists the
fruit of the Spirit in Galatians 5:22, 23, there is no ordering or numbering of the fruit as though its various facets
had rank, and there is no indication that the fruit is
differently distributed to different believers according
to the will of the Spirit. As we have already suggested,
this may be the significance of the cluster concept, that
in every believer's life all aspects of the fruit of the Spirit
will be manifest, whereas with the gifts of the Spirit,
there is a distribution according to the mind and the will
of the Spirit and undoubtedly in relationship to the
practical needs of the church for the fulfillment of its
gospel commission.

Another great principle governing the gifts of the
Spirit is that they must produce unity within the church

and be for the building up, or the edification of the church as a whole, for leading it on toward perfection in Christ Jesus. This the apostle makes abundantly clear as he discusses the matter with the Ephesian church when he says, "And his gifts were that some should be apostles, some prophets, some evangelists, some pastors and teachers, for the equipment of the saints, for the work of ministry, for building up the body of Christ, until we all attain the unity of the faith and of the knowledge of the Son of God, to mature manhood, to the measure of the stature of the fullness of Christ; so that we may no longer be children, tossed to and fro and carried about with every wind of doctrine, by the cunning of men, by their craftiness in deceitful wiles. Rather, speaking the truth in love, we are to grow up in every way into Him who is the head, into Christ, from whom the whole body, joined and knit together by every joint with which it is supplied, when each part is working properly, makes bodily growth and upbuilds itself in love." Ephesians 4:11-16, R.S.V.

Unless one wishes to take the position that the church has already reached the condition of maturity and unity which the apostle describes here, then there is continuing room for and need for the gifts of the Spirit. Throughout its history the Seventh-day Adventist Church has had the expectation of a special outpouring of the Holy Spirit's presence and power upon the church in the final thrust of the gospel commission to all the world. The fullness of power in proclaiming the everlasting gospel of Revelation 14:6-12 would surely bring, in connection with this "latter rain" bestowal of the Spirit, a revival of and perhaps even an addition to the gifts of the Spirit described and experienced in the New Testament church.

To the degree that today there are new circumstances and new conditions that were unknown to the New Testament church it is conceivable that the Holy Spirit might bestow gifts now that were not needed then. And certainly the Seventh-day Adventist Church needs to retain an openness to spiritual gifts. The apostle Paul told the Corinthians to seek the higher gifts and related that he himself had a number of these gifts and exercised them in his gospel work. There is nothing contradictory in the suggestion that the remnant church today should seek the Lord both for the fruit of the Spirit in ever-increasing measure in the life of each believer and for the gifts of the Spirit to be renewed to the church as the Spirit sees the need.

With the return to chaotic conditions in society, as in the days of Noah, and the difficulties of travel anticipated and the outbreak of disease and pestilence on an ever-widening scale, with the catastrophes of earthquakes and storms, anticipated as signs of the soon-returning Saviour, there could be as great a need for the gifts in the final thrust of the gospel message as there was in launching that gospel message at Pentecost and immediately thereafter. Perhaps the need now might be even greater. But here again the Corinthian church may give us warning that it is easy to become spiritually puffed up over spiritual gifts. There certainly is no indication of being puffed up over the fruit of the Spirit, when meekness is one of the characteristics. But it is so easy for the naturally selfish human heart to take credit to itself even for spiritual endowments, even for its humility, and to begin to make comparisons between and among ourselves and to exalt some gifts and belittle others and thus to create rifts in the church where the gifts of the Spirit were designed for the unity and upbuilding and maturity of the church of God on earth.

It would appear from the record that no one excelled the apostle Paul in devotion and sacrifice and achievement in the building up of the church of Jesus Christ. No one exceeded him in the reception of the gifts of the Spirit. He could tell the Corinthians that he spoke with tongues more than all of them. In his far-flung travels this could have been a very real need. Gifts of healing, of discernment, of administration, of evangelism and teaching were markedly his. He was perhaps the supreme apostle—perhaps receiving to a greater degree this first of all gifts of the Spirit (apostleship) than anyone else; and yet even toward the end of his life he could speak of himself as chief of sinners. Thus he indicated that he had not allowed his spiritual endowments in any way to become the basis or ground of his expectation of eternal life. He was ever mindful, as we have said before, that he had once persecuted the church of Jesus Christ; and nothing that the Lord did through him afterward seemed to be sufficient to erase from his memory, from his conscience, and from his heart the fact that he had wounded his Lord in the person of His church.

Can we not believe that God will yet manifest His gifts of the Spirit in connection with the final proclamation of the everlasting gospel in a manner beyond the expectation of any and all of us? He desires glory to be reflected to His own name by what He wishes to do and will ultimately do in and through His church. The entire gospel message and commission, with its intent to restore the whole man to the image of God, will be revived in its fullness, but it will be revived only as the love portrayed in First Corinthians 13 is revived. And the secret for that revival is the fruit of the Spirit in the life of every believer. When the fruit of the Spirit is seen in the life of every believer, the gifts of the Spirit will follow as God leads His remnant church on to final victory. Victory will come in calling God's true children out of every persuasion into the full life of the everlasting gospel of faith in Jesus Christ, a faith leading to obedience to all the commandments of God under the direction and guidance of the testimony of Jesus Christ. The greatest days of the church therefore are still in the future, when the gospel will finish in a blaze of glory that will exceed even the manifestation and effectiveness of the apostolic witness at the first Pentecost. God speed that day.

8.The Lord Our Righteousness

Through the prophet Jeremiah the prediction was made to both Judah and Israel that a Branch of the house of David should come to rule over God's people and would carry the title, "The Lord Our Righteousness." Jeremiah 23:6. He also predicted that the city of Jerusalem could benefit from the ministry of the Branch of Righteousness and itself carry the title "The Lord Our Righteousness." (See Jeremiah 33:16.) As we who can look back upon the New Testament are aware, neither Judah and Israel nor Jerusalem lived up to the divine promise and possibility in their response to the Branch of the house of David. Jesus Christ the Anointed One came of the house and line of David and was born in David's city; but, tragically, Jerusalem knew not the full significance of the day of her opportunity.

Even though the Lord rode into Jerusalem in a triumphal procession in which the spirit of prophecy came upon the common people and the children and the disciples of the Lord so that they proclaimed hosannas to the Son of David and fulfilled the divine predictions and gave honor to Him as their King, the leaders of the people and the majority of the people themselves were not prepared to accept the Lord on His own terms. Their long-standing traditions and their own national ambitions, in the face of the relentless domination of the Roman Empire, distorted their expectations of the Holy One of Israel. Therefore, when He came as He did—meek and lowly, without earthly pretention, without the symbols and signals of wealth and power, without military might and support—they could not accept Him. He did not meet their logically determined, rational expectation of what the Messiah must be in order to do what they had come to believe the Messiah should do. Had they examined carefully the total message of the prophets, which they had in their hands in the Old Testament, instead of selecting from the Old Testament predictions only those which suited their personal ideas and ambitions, they could have known, they could have recognized the Lord of Glory beneath the humble guise of the Man of Galilee.

Instead, God's chosen people continued through the round of services and ceremonies which were the externals of the system of worship entrusted to the Hebrew people by Jehovah. But the heart of those services was gone. The symbolic significance was no longer contemplated. There was an expectation of righteousness based upon works of primarily human devising and undertaking. In the ordained sacrificial system centered in the temple of Jerusalem few saw the shadow of things to come which the Lord had placed in them. So as the apostle Paul said, Israel, forgetting the righteousness which the Lord alone could give her, had gone about to create her own righteousness and had ended her endeavors in utter failure. (See Romans 10:1-4.)

Physical and historical Israel of old fell into the snare of attempting to establish her own righteousness in the place of the righteousness that comes only from God (and as represented by the substitutionary sacrifices which she had ever before her over the centuries). This fact gives occasion to sound a note of warning for spiritual Israel under the New Testament gospel. She likewise is in danger of falling into the snare of forgetting the righteousness which Christ alone can give and of attempting to establish her own righteousness in obedience to the laws of God through human will and effort.

As some of us have learned from personal experience, and as is clearly established in the history of the Seventh-day Adventist Church (particularly following the 1888 time of crisis and confrontation), it is perpetually easy to slip back into a pattern of counting on human efforts and works to be the basis, if only to some degree, for the salvation of the believer. It seems to run contrary to the desires of human nature, of human pride and independence and self-efficiency to acknowledge dependence. It is hard to rejoice in the knowledge that one is utterly dependent upon the righteousness of another to make oneself acceptable to God and to be counted as righteous before Him. If we could only believe the promises of God, there is nothing else designed to bring so great peace of mind and calm confidence under trial and provocation as the sweet and blessed assurance that the righteousness of Jesus is my righteousness. This is an amazing factor of human experience. Over the Seventh-day Adventist Church there needs to be flying today an unmistakable banner proclaiming "The Lord Our Righteousness."

Throughout this small volume we have expressed again and again in a score of different ways, from different approaches and by different illustrations, from different times and different peoples, that Christ is our

Substitute and our Surety, that He has taken our place, that He has gained our victory and is our overcomer, that He has made Himself our sacrifice, that He has taken the full consequences for our disobedience. When we place our wills in His hands and accept Him utterly as our Redeemer, as the One who stands in our place, our acceptance before God is made sure in Him who is our Surety. He becomes the guarantor of our acceptance with God, not because of works of righteousness which we have done but because of His works of perfect righteousness which He has done. Yet He has been treated as we deserve that we might be treated as He deserves.

The human heart keeps wanting to modify this sweet and blessed assurance in some way and in some degree. Even after casting our all upon Him, we seem to want to come sneaking back later and take some of the credit away from Him and to ourselves for our salvation and for our restoration to harmony and unity and acceptance with God. We just cannot seem to conclude that we are utterly and altogether and always dependent on Him and His righteousness for our salvation. We may even be tempted to think and even to express it that having accepted Him as our Substitute and Surety and having walked with Him for a while in paths of righteousness, in the way of sanctification, or the way of holiness, then we can begin to take a little of the credit to ourselves and feel less dependent upon Him and upon His righteousness counted to us for righteousness. We may think, even if we don't say it, that we have become less dependent upon His justifying righteousness because of our growth in grace on the road of sanctification.

Perhaps there could be a limited and special sense in which such a view of the relationship between justification and sanctification could be understandable, in the sense that however feeble or strong our best intentions and efforts to do the will of God, Christ stands ready to make up the deficit with and by His own righteousness, and we might hope that the deficit is growing smaller as we grow in grace. But in another sense it could be extremely dangerous to entertain such a concept, because there seems to be no inspired instruction as to how one would know when or whether he himself or anyone else had finally reached Christ's perfect ideal for His children. If sanctification is the work of a lifetime, then, in such an ongoing work, would it not be dangerous to contemplate a stopping point where one would feel (even if he did not say it aloud), that he had now reached, shall we say, a state of sinlessness?,

If we were *forced* to make a choice as to which is more important to our salvation, justification or sanctification, we would have to give that distinction to justification. The righteousness by which we are accounted righteous is flawless. It is the righteousness of Jesus Christ Himself, produced nearly two thousand years ago. The righteousness by which we are sanctified is imparted to us here and now by Jesus Christ through the ministry of the Holy Spirit, but it is the righteousness which is in us, who are still in our sinful flesh and subject to temptations, and we do fall. So there is no point in time when we can claim that we have full, complete, perfect righteousness. Even our prayers are touched by human weakness and frailty and must be sent heavenward with the incense of Christ's righteousness. Sanctification is growth, the work of the whole life, the fight to maintain a relationship—it is the fruit of justification, the result, the product, and cannot have priority over justification.

I recall very early in my student ministry days meet-

An awareness of what Christ has done in becoming our peace, our Saviour leads us to respond in repentance.

ing a member of the church who assured me that for a period of some three years she had not sinned. This attitude and self-evaluation process is fraught with extreme peril, if only because it tends to direct the focus of attention and of confidence inward upon the self. It is true that the Lord calls upon us to search our hearts as with a candle for every trace of sin, that sin might be expelled from the soul through the power and mercy of Jesus Christ. But to look inward with the thought of self-congratulations or self-confidence is to run the risk of turning the gaze away from Him who is the Author and the Finisher of our faith. (See Hebrews 12:1, 2.)

No patriarch, prophet, or apostle ever claimed to have reached the point of perfection, the place of sinlessness. On the contrary we find those who walked with the Lord the longest—and may we dare to say the closest—were the most consistent in protesting their own utter dependence on the righteousness of the Lord counted to them for righteousness—whether we want to think of Daniel confessing his sins with the sins of his people Israel, or of the apostle Paul classing himself as chief of sinners, or of the beloved apostle John declaring "if we say that we have no sin, we deceive ourselves, and the truth is not in us." "If we say that we have not sinned, we make him a liar, and his word is not in us." 1 John 1:8, 10.

That there will ultimately be a body of believers on the face of this earth in its present state and age who will actually be found "spotless" is a Scriptural teaching and expectation. (See Revelation 14:5, R.S.V.) But how or when that body of believers will *know* that they have reached that condition is nowhere made plain in the counsels of the Lord, and it does not run contrary to our reason to see why that might have to be. For until our human nature in its mortal and fallen state and condi-

tion has been transformed by the final act of God, causing this mortal to put on immortality and this corrupti-
ble to put on incorruption, and as long as there is an evil
one to tempt and seduce us, it would be extremely
dangerous for any follower of the Lord to feel that he has
made all necessary achievements and growth and that
he can relax his vigil, as it were, and coast his way into
the eternal kingdom.

Just the opposite seems to be the consistent picture
portrayed for us through the Scriptures and the counsels
of the Lord's Spirit. We gain the impression repeatedly
that as long as we are in this flesh, we shall have temptation to overcome and self to subdue and an adversary to
resist. The closer also that we actually come to the Lord
the more we shall sense the awfulness of sin, including
our own sins, and the more we shall loathe them and
loathe ourselves for having committed them, just as the
apostle loathed himself throughout his life for having
once persecuted the church of Jesus Christ.

But this very growing and increasing sensitivity to the
sinfulness of sin drives the believer to depend the more
heavily upon the justifying righteousness of Christ
counted to him for righteousness, so that, when the
Judge of all the earth begins to recite to the redeemed all
that they have done for Him, they find it difficult to
believe. They are unconscious of their works of righteousness and Christlikeness. Their minds have been
filled with the yearning to do and to be much more—
never satisfied except in the satisfaction which Christ
has provided for all the requirements of God pertaining
to their salvation.

But someone says, "Are we not likely to grow careless
of what we say and what we do when we are trusting
solely in the merits of another to stand in our place?"

That is undoubtedly possible, for many claim the name of Jesus and claim His righteousness who have no sense of the holy nature of God's law or of the sinfulness of their own nature or of heaven's distaste for the sins which they commit. Some of the same are quick to accuse as legalists those who are concerned to do the will of the Lord in every small detail known to them. There are those who boast of their freedom in the righteousness of Christ so that they do not have to be concerned to observe the Sabbath carefully, to eat and drink solely to the glory of God, to be careful what the ears hear and the eyes behold, because say they, "I am covered with the righteousness of Jesus."

That there is not the slightest support for this attitude anywhere in Scripture should be abundantly clear to any who would care to investigate. Listen to the beloved John when he says, "He that saith I know him, and keepeth not his commandments, is a liar, and the truth is not in him. But whoso keepeth his word, in him verily is the love of God perfected: hereby know we that we are in him." "He that keepeth his commandments dwelleth in him, and he in him." 1 John 2:4, 5; 3:24. And Peter and Paul and James echo the same truth.

He who has his eye of faith on Calvary's cross, he who contemplates what his Lord endured for him in Gethsemane and on Calvary, he who remembers that when the believer sins he crucifies the Lord afresh and puts Him to an open shame—such a man can never take a light or careless view of sin, no matter what its form. The apostle John again made the situation so clear. "You know that he appeared to take away sins," he said, "and in him there is no sin. No one who abides in him sins; no one who sins has either seen him or known him." 1 John 3:5, 6, R.S.V.

132

There are those who stumble in the opposite direction over these words from John, for these people assert that anyone who has sinned demonstrates thereby that he has never been born again and that he is not truly one of God's children. We have to remember that John who wrote the words quoted above had already indicated at the beginning of his letter that "if we say we have no sin, we deceive ourselves, and the truth is not in us." Also he had said, "If we say we have not sinned, we make him a liar, and his word is not in us." He continued by saying, "My little children, I am writing this to you so that you may not sin." 1 John 1:8, 10; 2:1, R.S.V.

Notice that it is John's purpose to show the believers, followers of the Lord Jesus Christ, who are addressed with terms of endearment by the apostle, that they should not sin. He instructs them on how to relate to the Lord so that sin shall have less and less sway in their lives. But even as he says: "I am writing this to you so that you may not sin," he continues by saying, "but if anyone does sin, we have an advocate with the Father, Jesus Christ the righteous." And just a few sentences earlier he had assured these same dear children that, "If we confess our sins, he is faithful and just, and will forgive our sins and cleanse us from all unrighteousness." 1 John 2:1; 1:9, R.S.V.

What is the spiritual condition of the church that professes to be entrusted with God's last warning message to the world before Jesus returns? According to the messages from Jesus to the seven churches of Revelation, the church of which we are a part is characterized by Laodicea, a church which is unaware of its real spiritual need; a church that is satisfied with its present attainments and spiritual experience; a church that is actually lukewarm but doesn't seem to know it; a church that is blind spiritually but seems unaware of its blindness; a church that is naked and is unaware of its ungainly and undesirable appearance; a church that is wretched and poor and yet thinks all along that it is rich and that all is well. It is utterly impossible to conceive a greater contradiction or a greater self-deception than that which the Laodicean church has brought upon itself. And the one who alone can meet the real needs of the church (if it only knew what those needs are) is left standing at the door knocking, knocking and desiring to come in and wanting to come in, being willing to come in, but actually kept waiting outside the door.

We may individually console ourselves that this is a general characteristic of the whole church and does not apply to us personally. But it is interesting that in the Revelation the portrayal seems to be that of the Lord knocking at the heart of an individual rather than the hearts of a group. One of God's most faithful servants among our pioneers expressed great gratitude for the simple steps which the Lord has revealed to us by which we may come to Him. She asked on one occasion why it was that so many claimed that it was so hard to find the Lord. How could it be so hard to find Him when He is standing at the door of your heart knocking, knocking, knocking? Where would you go to look for Him, to search for Him? In the forests, on the mountainside, in the cave? He is just outside your heart's door. He has everything you need, the robe of His own righteousness with which to cover the shame of your nakedness and your filthy rags of self-righteousness. He has eyesalve that will heal your spiritual blindness so that you can perceive and discern between good and evil, truth and error, righteousness and unrighteousness. He has gold, an abundance of gold—the gold of faith and love with which to counteract your impoverished and wretched condition. And laden with these very necessities of yours, He stands at the door knocking, knocking. He cannot come in unless and until you open the door. He has no key to your will. That is in your hands alone. Why don't you go to the door and open it and say, "Come in, dear Lord, come in. I love you, and I want to obey your will." Don't expect Him to find your heart in the condition that it needs to be. If it were, you wouldn't need Him. Remember the prayer of the hymn writer, "Come not to find but make this troubled room a dwelling worthy of Thee as Thou art."

The Lord is waiting to send His remnant people forth to the world with the banner of the everlasting gospel proclaiming the indivisible harmony and unity of the commandments of God and the faith of Jesus, but He cannot do it until He has a people willing to move out under the banner which proclaims to the world, "The Lord Our Righteousness."

9. Our Merciful High Priest

At several points in the previous chapters reference has been made to the mediatorial work of Jesus Christ. He offers the prayers of His followers to the heavenly Father, sweetened with the incense of His own righteousness and sprinkled with the precious blood of His own atoning sacrifice. It has been seen that the New Testament believer in Jesus Christ is relating to the heavenly reality of our great High Priest as the worshipers at the temple of ancient Israel related to the miniature, earthly representation of the heavenly sanctuary and to the priesthood that ministered there daily and yearly.

It seems appropriate, therefore, to consider a little more fully the role of Jesus as our High Priest and to review how the Seventh-day Adventist Church understands this ministry.

Although many Bible students, of all faiths, over the centuries have been aware that Christ is Mediator between God and man, Seventh-day Adventists have maintained a unique interest in this phase of Christ's Messiahship and see it as an integral aspect of the total plan of salvation guaranteed by the Lord our righteousness and one which has special end-time significance.

In the early nineteenth century there developed a worldwide expectation of a soon return of Jesus Christ in fulfillment of the promise of the angel to the apostles at Christ's ascension to heaven: "This Jesus, who was taken up from you into heaven, will come in the same way as you saw him go into heaven." Acts 1:11, R.S.V. This expectation was the direct result of the study of prophetic portions of the Scriptures (the books of Daniel and Revelation especially) and particularly the coming of the "time of the end" foretold in both books. With the independent calculation and publication by a number of Bible students (as early as 1700) that the 1260 days, (years) of "little horn" power would terminate "around 1800" (1798, to be more precise) and that this terminus would mark the beginning of the "time of the end," the Advent expectation began to mount. (See Daniel 7:24-28; cf. Revelation 12:14; 11:3.)

Not only did this time prophecy of 1260 days (years) stir expectation, but with confirming events coming to pass in 1798 (as predicted nearly a century earlier), attention turned to the still unexplained and apparently unfulfilled longer period of 2300 days (years) of Daniel 8:14, predicting the time for the beginning of the cleansing of the sanctuary.

By the use of identical interpretation principles as had applied to the 1260 day prophecies, the year 1843-1844 was projected for the time at which "the sanctuary [would] be cleansed." Study turned to the sanctuary and its cleansing, most fully described in Leviticus 16 in the Old Testament. The types and symbols there described were seen as having been, and also yet to be, fulfilled by Jesus Christ, as described in the book of Hebrews in the New Testament. A comparative study of these Scriptures (Leviticus and Hebrews), together with the books of Daniel and Revelation and the gospel accounts, led to the belief that the earth (sanctuary) would be cleaned up by fire (cleansed) at the coming of the Lord in 1843-1844 (unto 2300 days or years).

Going back to Christ's role as Mediator, let it be noted that the apostle Paul had written to Timothy that "there is one mediator between God and man, the Man Christ Jesus" (1 Timothy 2:5). The writer of the Hebrews (also widely accepted as Paul) portrays Christ as the Mediator of the new (and better) covenant, by virtue of His own blood which He has shed. (See Hebrews 8:6; 9:15-22.) A mediator (Gk. *mesitēs*) was and is a middleman. As seen throughout the previous chapters of this present volume, Christ has been portrayed as living man's life, dying his death, and becoming his Substitute and Surety before the Father, at whose right hand He has been installed. There He applies to penitent believers the benefits of the purchased atonement which He completed at Calvary by shedding His own righteous blood on the cross. (See Acts 7:54-56; 2:32-36; John 17:11.)

In these respects Christ has purchased the right to be our middleman, our Mediator between God and man. By His divinity He has right to the throne of heaven, and by His humanity He is in living contact and relationship with and to us. He is the mystical ladder seen in Jacob's dream on which the heavenly messengers have the right to ascend and descend in their ceaseless ministry between God and man. (See Genesis 28:10-17, Hebrews 1:14.)

The great creeds of the Christian church have long recognized the reality of Christ's mediatorial work in heaven, since His ascension, from whence they have looked for Him to return at His second coming, not to make a sacrifice for sins this time, but to sit in judgment upon men, according as each one has esteemed or despised (even ignored or neglected) the means which Heaven has provided at infinite cost for man's salvation. As noted earlier, this is what Christ explained to Nicodemus in their night-shrouded interview. (See John 3:16-21.)

Before Seventh-day Adventists emerged as a remnant from the great advent awakening of the early 1800s, Bible believers by the scores of thousands, all over the Christian world, were studying Christ's high-priestly work in the sanctuary in heaven (of which sanctuary Moses was given instruction to make a miniature, portable model in the wilderness around Sinai, and of which Solomon built a more glorious and permanent imitation in a temple to the Lord).

These Christian "advent" believers saw their Lord as completing His work in the heavens as High Priest Mediator (after the pattern of the intercessory work of the Old Testament sanctuary/temple high priests) and coming as King of kings temporarily clad in garments of vengeance to cleanse the earth of sin and sinners, and to make new heavens and new earth, wherein righteousness would dwell. (For detailed study, see F. D. Nichol, *The Midnight Cry*; and L. E. Froom, *The Prophetic Faith of Our Fathers.*)

As the strength of the worldwide advent awakening ebbed and flowed, the Old World expectation dissipated in concern over speaking in tongues and in seeing the Jews accept the gospel and return to Palestine. But the New World expectation intensified even as that in the Old World dimmed, and the Millerite Movement (named after William Miller, a farmer/militiaman/Bible-prophecy student) gave increasing attention to the Old Testament types, symbols, and ceremonies associated with the earthly wilderness sanctuary.

It was the Millerites especially (although there were key witnesses overseas) who concentrated on the study of the 2300 days (years) of prophecy of Daniel 8:14 and the predicted cleansing of the sanctuary. So careful was their study that by Jewish calendation they fixed a number of intervening events located within the 2300-year span and determined its beginning and then its terminal point with increasing care and accuracy.

When the much-heralded and much-despised day for the Lord's return passed without the expected fulfillment, most of the adherents were prepared to steal away and hide. But a remnant could not deny the sweet genuineness of their experience of expectation and the marked presence of the Spirit of Christ among them as they gave their "final" appeals to sinners.

Only in imagination can we conceive how the calculated and long-awaited joy of the climactic event on the "tenth day of the seventh month" (Jewish reckoning) turned to the bitterness of disappointment and crushing humiliation when no visible glory of the returning Christ split the heavens. Most of the disappointed ones turned away from their past confidence and abandoned their view of the termination of the 2300 days. But again a remnant clung to the Lord in faith that there must be a reason for their experience.

In response to earnest prayer, the Spirit of Truth guided them back to a more careful consideration of the sanctuary types and to the description of their very experience in Revelation 10:8-11. They saw in the sanctuary types that a final work of testing, verifying the faith of believers—a kind of judgment by evaluation— would terminate the work of the heavenly Mediator and immediately precede His advent.

With clarifying understanding and the directing manifestation of spiritual gifts among them (1 Corinthians 12; Ephesians 4) they began to speak and teach of Christ's final work of mediation in the heavenly sanctuary as the antitype of the final annual work of the high priest in the earthly sanctuary/temple on the day of atonement (Yom Kippur)—a solemn day of afflicting the soul for sin, a day of faith, of dedication, of judgment, of separation, and of deliverance.

The thickening signs of the Lord's soon return encourage those who trust in His righteousness and submit to His will to expect with eager anticipation their union with Him soon. However, there is always a solemnizing sense in which the nearness of His appearing leads them to ask themselves: "Am I ready? Is my lamp trimmed and burning? Are all known sins confessed, forsaken? Is there restitution to be made to those wronged in any way? Is it my supreme priority to be ready and to help others be ready for the return of the Bridegroom?"

The ancient Day of Atonement was a time for Israel to put aside all secular activity, to gather about the sanctuary in solemn searching of heart for the confession and abandonment of sin and for renewed demonstration of trust in the effectiveness of the sacrifice made for sin. In prayer and hope they waited for the return of the High Priest from the most holy place where was kept God's sacred law of love—the law written on tables of stone and placed beneath the seat of mercy. So today those who recognize the final work of Jesus as their Mediator before the law and throne of God await with solemn trust His return, with the cares of this life relegated to a secondary place.

It is against this background that Seventh-day Adventists have spoken of the atoning work of Jesus Christ in the heavenly sanctuary since His ascension—and in a final setting since 1844. The price of redemption was all paid in full at Calvary—"It is finished"—but the application of the blood to each penitent believer is the continuing ministry of Jesus, our Mediator. (See Hebrews 7:26, 27; 8:1, 2, 5; 9:11-14, 24-28.)

So the noble saints of past ages sleep in the momentary (to them) silence of death until the final battles have been won, the final generation tested and found true. The work of investigation to determine which professed followers of Jesus by faith in His atonement and genuine repentance of sin are entitled to the benefits of His atonement has been completed. (See Hebrews 11:39, 40.)

"So Christ, having been offered once to bear the sins of many, will appear a second time, not to deal with sin but to save those who are eagerly waiting for him." Hebrews 9:28, R.S.V.

Thus, with all true Bible-following Christians, Seventh-day Adventists have a backward and a forward look—back to the cross where the price was paid, and forward to the day of His soon appearing at the completion of His High-priestly, mediatorial work at the Father's right hand.

10. I Shall Be Whole

Just in case the reader may by now have forgotten the setting of the "Prologue" to this volume, and the basic issues which it illustrated, we should perhaps add an epilogue to bring us back full circle to our starting point and to review the Newbold experience in the light of our discoveries in the Written Word of God, the Bible.

There has been abundant and consistent biblical support for the experience of entering into and receiving from God justification—being counted righteous—by faith in the righteousness of Jesus Christ which is counted to the penitent, believing, born-again child of God for righteousness. He then stands before God in the righteousness of Christ, and the Father accepts the justified one as though he had never sinned. (This book has been able to gather only some of the *highlights* of the biblical evidence.)

The Bible perfectly understands the earnest desire of the justified believer to have everyone know of the peace of soul that has come to him—a peace which passes all understanding—a peace that flows deep and steady, for it is based not on the good works or merits of the believer but upon the perfect and unchanging merits of the sinless Lamb of God.

142

The Bible understands the desire of those "justified" Newbold students to do whatever God had revealed or would reveal to be His will. It understands their new-found love for the law of God, for Jesus had removed their condemnation before the law, had shown them that His righteousness perfectly fulfills and exemplifies that eternal law which is a transcript of the character of God. Those young people saw in Jesus Christ, as never before, a perfect reflection of the law of God.

Moreover, the Bible sees newly justified believers (students or otherwise) as newly grafted-in branches of Jesus Christ, the True Vine. It sees the heavenly Father-Gardener bending over His vine tenderly, using the testing, painful pruning knife only to enhance the development of the fruit of the Spirit in the branches of the vine. His glory is enhanced by the measure of their fruitfulness.

The Newbold students found a new depth of joy in and motivation for the study of the Bible and the counsels of the Spirit to the remnant church. And that, too, is what the Bible endorses. It is Christ's plea that His words shall abide in His branches, as they abide in Him.

Ten-league strides (with some stumbling) in the path toward holiness, Christlikeness, sanctification, were taken by those newly justified young people. Theirs was not an on-again off-again relationship to Jesus Christ. And the Word understands that. The *only* requirement of the branches is that they shall *abide* in the vine. Then the promise is that the vine will abide in them. What activity! What restfulness! The inclination of Jesus Christ to bear the fruit of the Spirit is now dwelling in, surging through, transforming them.

For busy college students, the prayer meeting became a joy; the testimony meeting, a precious opportunity to share newfound depths of love and peace in the righteousness of Jesus Christ. The Bible understands that. "Then they that feared the Lord spake often one to another."

Well, the years have scattered and separated those schoolmates of an earlier generation at the original Newbold College (named for the old mansion, Newbold Revel, that was the heart and extent of the school). They have served in different lands, in different capacities. And only the Lord Himself knows the degree to which they still retain the peace that justification brought them over thirty years ago.

One thing is sure. If they have taken the focus of their spiritual gaze away from the accounted righteousness of Jesus (justifying righteousness), and have begun to lean the weight of their hope for eternal life upon their self-measured progress in the path of sanctification, then their peace and joy in the Lord may have dimmed. If they have come to measure and weigh their individual fruit-bearing results, and have begun to place their confidence in these, rather than in the acceptability to God of the life-giving True Vine, then they have fallen back into a self-centered rather than a Christ-centered confidence. Such a confidence cannot endure, though it may deceive. The fruit borne will not be the fruit of the Spirit.

It has been a source of perplexity and disappointment to some who were involved in the "Prologue" experience, that the church at large has not even yet entered into the fullness of peace and joy and power that comes with the justifying righteousness of Jesus Christ. The reticence of 1888 is with the church yet. We are still afraid of putting all our weight on the imputed righteousness of Christ. We are afraid that in doing so we shall do an injustice to the law of God, promote cheap grace, encourage a drift toward the lowered moral standards of the world about us.

Such reluctance cannot be a valid fear for the believer who begins every day with a renewed recognition that his "hope is built on nothing less than Jesus' blood and righteousness." He cannot see His Saviour again in Gethsemane, again on Calvary's hill, lifted up between earth and heaven, and know that the Lord was there in order to provide him with *His* righteousness—he cannot do these things and take a light view of sin which is the transgression of God's law. Such a man is converted every day. Self dies daily, self is daily crucified. To him the cross says, "Higher yet!" The law says, "Higher yet!" The example of Jesus says, "Higher yet!" And the engrafted branch of the True Vine says, "Even so, Lord. Higher yet, and higher yet. And thank You, Lord. In You I am complete, Your righteousness is mine! And I am chief of sinners. None of self, and all of Thee!"

The most terrible and yet the most awesome days of the church are still ahead. The conflict of the ages moves to its climax. Clad in the armor of Christ's righteousness, bearing in abundance the fruit of the Spirit, endowed with the gifts of the Spirit for the work of giving the final call of the everlasting gospel, reflecting more and more completely the image of her Lord, yet becoming even more and more aware of her own sinfulness and helplessness, the church justified and being sanctified, moves out for the final encounter with the enemy of God and man—the enemy who said from the beginning of his rebellion, "I will exalt myself"—moves out to give the final warning, the last call of a God of mercy to a world that careens on to chaos and destruction.

With climactic power the church proclaims with "a loud cry" what the devil has never wanted men to know—the righteous God who loves righteousness and hates iniquity has provided for you the garments of *His* righteousness, the heavenly wedding garment purchased by the cross and by the life of Jesus. Will you accept it? Will you wear it? It is your only hope. It is your last chance. No, you cannot improve on it, cannot buy it, cannot adapt it. Will you receive the gift of heaven? Will you believe God? Will you trust His promises? Will you keep His commandments? Will you escape from the wrath to come? Will you make Him Lord of your life?

Over the church, over the marching triumphant saints, over the eternal city of God, over the hosts of the redeemed, over the eleventh-hour victors who respond to the last call, flies a banner, the gospel banner, the banner of eternal victory, the banner—"The Lord Our Righteousness."

My friend, the Lord is passing close by even as you read these words. He has everything you need for eternal life. Have you let Him heal you of the fountain of sin and uncleanness that is in your soul? Dare you wait for a "more convenient season"? Remember the woman who touched the hem of His garment. You, too, can be made whole!

I Shall Be Whole

On the swirling fringes of the curious crowd
    she was swept along—
        a nameless face,
        a feeble body, steadily growing more feeble.

What if the crushing crowd, now bearing her along,
    should let her sink, exhausted, to the dust—
        the searing, choking dust—
    should trample heedless feet upon her prostrate form,
    should forsake her as an unclaimed clump of lifeless rags?

The sense of threatening danger penetrated her nausea,
        roused her dizzying brain,
          clarified her thoughts,
until her lips formed anew her oft-repeated pledge:
        I SHALL BE WHOLE.

It was not that she spoke the words to anybody,
        for who would believe her?
          Who would listen?
    Indeed, had she not come to question whether she could believe
        herself?

Had not twelve relentless years of searing pain—
        of hope renewed to be destroyed,
          renewed to be destroyed again, and yet again—
had they not made hope well-nigh hopeless?
But somewhere—somewhere in this crowd,
            this jostling, contentious, kaleidoscopic crowd,
          walks a new Physician
    and on Him rests her reemerging hope.

It had not been easy to believe the stories the neighbors told,
        of miracles performed, for high and low,
            for poor and rich,
          without respect to person.
But steadily the evidence had mounted, broadened then, and
        deepened,
   till from the dust of disappointment,
          disillusion,
           destitution,
  Faith had called forth hope's assertion:
        I SHALL BE WHOLE!

But now, here in the crowd, Faith falters,
          Hope hesitates,
          Trust trembles.
Could He who restored the widow's dead son,
    He who healed the leper by the sea,
    He who stilled death-waves on Galilee,
    He who mastered demons at Gergesa,

Could *He* not know that she, in whom His power had kindled hope,
    was seeking Him, oh, so desperately in this cruel crush?

Perhaps she never should have left the sanctuary of humble home,
    never should have contended with the seaside crowd,
    never should have dragged herself, pain-bowed,
        to Levi-Matthew's house,
  only to find that doors which shut the Healer in
      shut her out.
And now, if what she hears is right, Jairus, Ruler of the Synagogue,
    does with the Master walk and talk.
    And she? Who is she? What hope has she?

Cruel cynicism, punctuated by stabbing pain,
    underlined by the memory of twelve bitter years,
  batters at the citadel of faith within her heart.
And this indifferent crowd! Can she contend much more?
Yet from this very crowd she gathers wisps of conversation
      as the people eddy about her:
      "... fancy eating with publicans ..."
      "... enemy of our people."
        "He healed my child. ..."
    "... know where He's going now?"
        "... child of Jairus ... sick ... dying."
"... going to heal her ..."   "... Too late. ... Dead."
    "... going anyway. Remember the son at Nain."
It is enough. Her citadel of faith still stands,
      fortified with evidence anew.
  This is still the Man she needs to see.
With faith trial-tested, she proclaims to herself as true:

I SHALL BE WHOLE.
"But if only I could see Him.
"If only I could find . . ."
And there He is! Suddenly! The Man of her long quest,
            Hope of all her hopes.
    Why, she could touch Him—if she dared.
    Why, if she spoke to Him, He would hear her!
            He is close enough.
But her pounding heart will not permit the words to come,
        her breath supports no sound.
    And too, there is that man Jairus, Ruler of the Synagogue.

But the crowd—the crowd is closing in;
        about to rob her of her golden moment,
            the chance that might never come again.
The faith of her life is compressed into deliberate,
            conscious, consuming action.
She presses forward, reaching—reaching desperately through the
        crowd,
        and saying to herself, more strongly:
    "If I may but touch His garment,
        I shall be whole."
She only touched the hem of His garment,
        but in that instant, twelve dreary years of pain
            and feebleness were gone.
Her faith vindicated, her trust in the Lord confirmed,
    her one boon granted, her soul overflowing with gratitude,
            and the love of God,
    she is now ready to commit her nameless self to the curious
        crowd.

But there are no eddies, no movements of the crowd,
        to cover her retreat.
        Movement has ceased.
The Lord stands still; His disciples stand still; even Jairus
          and the crowd are still.
  And the Lord is looking, intently toward her.
  And the Lord is asking, "Who touched me?"
A murmur of merriment and surprise ripples through the crowd,
    and one disciple protests the folly of the question
        in *such* a crowd.

But the Lord does not change His purpose,
        does not shift His gaze;
     persists with His question, as He says,
"Somebody hath touched me:
    for I perceive that virtue is gone out of me."
Finding concealment vain, the nameless woman—
    her radiant countenance bejeweled with swift-falling tears
        of grateful joy—
     casts herself at the Saviour's feet,
    pours forth the story of her hidden healing.

For all time it must be known that the touch of the pressing crowd
      upon Christ's person, was *casual;*
        that the touch of the nameless woman,
      even upon His garment, was *casual;*
        that God's believing children
      are to declare His goodness.
And the divine benediction fell:
"Daughter, be of good comfort:

thy faith hath made thee whole;
     go in peace."

Jesus Christ is in our midst today.
  He is not far from any one of us.
    But the crowd,   the world,   is closing in.
May not today offer the final chance of healing?

Whatever the past, whatever the need,
          reach for Him now through the crowd, saying,
      "If I may but touch His garment,
        I SHALL BE WHOLE!"

Gordon M. Hyde, "I Shall Be Whole," *These Times* 75 (November 1966):10-12.

L.M.BASSETT

MARCH
1978